ANAHEIM

"Partners in Progress" by Cynthia Simone
Photo research by Laura Cordova Molmud
Produced in cooperation with the Anaheim Chamber of Commerce

Windsor Publications, Inc.
Chatsworth, California

ANAHEIM

City of Dreams

AN ILLUSTRATED HISTORY BY JOHN WESTCOTT

Windsor Publications, Inc.—History Books Division
Managing Editor: Karen Story
Design Director: Alexander D'Anca
Photo Director: Susan L. Wells
Executive Editor: Pamela Schroeder

Staff for *Anaheim: City of Dreams*
Manuscript Editor: Susan M. Pahle
Photo Editor: Robin Mastrogeorge Sterling
Senior Editor, Corporate Biographies: Judith Hunter
Production Editor, Corporate Biographies: Justin Scupine
Proofreader: Mary Jo Scharf
Customer Service Manager: Phyllis Feldman-Schroeder
Editorial Assistants: Dominique Jones, Kim Kievman,
    Michael Nugwynne, Kathy B. Peyser, Theresa J. Solis
Publisher's Representatives, Corporate Biographies:
    Cece Hernandez-Helmers and Todd Inder Muehle
Designer: Ellen Ifrah
Layout Artist, Corporate Biographies: Trish Meyer
Layout Artist, Editorial: Michael Burg

Windsor Publications, Inc.
Elliot Martin, Chairman of the Board
James L. Fish III, Chief Operating Officer
Michele Sylvestro, Vice President/Sales-Marketing
Mac Buhler, Vice President/Sponsor Acquisition

Library of Congress Cataloging-in-Publication Data:
Westcott, John, 1954-
    Anaheim : city of dreams : an illustrated history / by John Westcott.
        Partners in progress by Cynthia Simone ; produced in cooperation
        with Anaheim Chamber of Commerce. — 1st ed.
    p. 128 cm. 22x28
    Includes bibliographical references and index.
    ISBN 0-89781-354-5 : $25.95
    1. Anaheim (Calif.)—History. 2. Anaheim (Calif.)—Description—Views.
        3. Anaheim (Calif.)—Industries. I. Simone, Cynthia. Partners in prog-
        ress. 1990. II. Anaheim Chamber of Commerce. III. Title.
F869.A53W47   1990   90-38858
976.4'96—dc20   CIP

Contents

Acknowledgments

As solitary an effort as writing a book often seems, an author can never truly go it alone. And so it is with this history of Anaheim, for which many people graciously gave of their time and information.

Among them are Paul Apodaca of the Bowers Museum who granted his time and valued advice without hesitation. I also thank the librarians at the Elizabeth J. Schultz Local History Room at the Anaheim Public Library, and Ann Harder of the Santa Ana Public Library's local history room, for their assistance in finding the many books, clippings, and documents needed to get a glimpse of Anaheim's past.

I also want to thank all those, living and dead, whose invaluable books and articles on the history of Anaheim made the writing of this book possible, especially the late Leo J. Friis, who wrote so copiously and so accurately on the city's beginnings.

I could not leave out Susan Pahle, editor at Windsor Publications, for her work in editing the text or Herbert Pruett, who reviewed the text. Last but certainly not least, I thank my wife Pamela for her undying patience in coping with a "lost husband" for so many months.

Well-dressed Sunday school children pose with their teachers in front of the Anaheim First Presbyterian Church in 1893. Courtesy, Anaheim Public Library

Introduction

The title of this illustrated history of Anaheim was not chosen because the city is a fantasyland of dreams that always come true. No city is truly that, and like any other, Anaheim has had its share of broken dreams and disappointments.

What has set Anaheim apart from others has been its boldness, the willingness of civic leaders to eschew the caution and leap into projects they had no business getting into. Such brashness didn't always pay off; efforts to industrialize Anaheim in the 1920s, for example, failed miserably after the Ku Klux Klan tainted local politics. But

line of dreamers, going back to the German vintners who took a dry land filled with cactus and sagebrush and transformed it into the top grape-producing center in the state. They called Anaheim the "Mother Colony" because it was a community of beginnings, a theme that would be played out again and again over its history. The many "firsts" include becoming the first incorporated city of present-day Orange County and creating the first planning commission in the state.

The story of Anaheim, which also includes the Indians and rancheros who

The 1905 Anaheim City Band enlivened the community by performing at various functions throughout the town. Courtesy, Anaheim Public Library

it succeeded often enough to make Anaheim a unique city indeed. What other municipality of its size—about 244,000 as the 1980s ended—could claim Disneyland, the largest convention center on the West Coast, and two major professional sports teams within its borders? Such facilities are only the latest claims of a city with a long

dwelled in the area long before there was a city, also demonstrates a fact too often forgotten in Southern California, that the region has a long and fascinating history, filled with heroes and villains and unexpected twists and turns. And Anaheim's story is as rich and fascinating—and instructive—as that of any city in Southern California.

Because of the mild climate and the abundance of the land, the Juaneño and Gabrielino tribes of today's Orange County and south Los Angeles County were able to spend a significant portion of their daily lives pursuing artistic, cultural, and spiritual endeavors. Villages for both of these enlightened tribes could be found in the Anaheim area. Courtesy, Historical Collection, First American Title Insurance Company

A Land Untamed

Archaeological evidence indicates the first Native American inhabitants in the Anaheim area were here at least 20,000 years ago. Some time before, these immigrants ended their long migration from Asia and found a land where the climate was mild and dry and where game was plentiful. They settled by the Santa Ana River, flowing from the mountains of the same name. Often the river shrunk to only a trickle, eventually disappearing underground in the sandy soil. But in heavy rains it fanned out across the valley, depositing the soil that would later grow grapes and Valencia oranges.

Some 4,000 years ago, a new wave of Indians arrived who shared linguistic roots with the Shoshone tribe. As time went by, a huge wedge of Southern California Indians, from Santa Barbara to Oceanside, adapted the language of the newcomers, but the culture and lifestyle of the original inhabitants remained intact and was accepted by the new groups of Indians.

Early Europeans portrayed Southern Californian Indians as primitive and lacking in culture and technology. We now know that was far from the truth. Because of the mild climate and the wealth of the land, the Indians only had to spend about four hours a day to maintain their lifestyle; the rest of the time was left for cultural, religious, and artistic endeavors, and there is evidence of all three.

Southern California Indians are credited with some of the finest basketry in the world, including baskets coated with pitch that could carry water. They followed the movement of sun, moon, and stars and kept calendars. They also made the only wood-planked canoes known in pre-European North America.

The early inhabitants of the Anaheim area consisted of two tribes whose descendants are still found in today's Orange County and south Los Angeles County. Dominating the southern portion of Orange County were the Acacgmemem. North Orange County and south Los Angeles County were the domain of the Atilililipish. Both tribes are better known by the names the Spaniards gave them: Acacgmemem became Juaneños, for their assignment to Mission San Juan Capistrano, and Atilililipish became Gabrielinos, for Mission San Gabriel. There was no firm dividing line between the two tribes, and the villages of both could be found in the Anaheim area.

Juaneños and Gabrielinos were scattered in villages throughout the area, each village consisting of a few hundred members or less. Men hunted for deer and other game; lobster was readily available off the coast. The women collected wild seeds and acorns, ground them into meal, and then made gruel.

For both Juaneños and Gabrielinos, religion played an important role in everyday life. Early Juaneño mythology centered on Wiyot, who was the first man and who represented human experience. Beyond that was what the Juaneños and virtually all Indian tribes regarded as "the Great Mystery," which dealt with eternal questions such as how the world was created. No attempt was made to explain it.

What we know of Juaneño mythology comes from the essay "Chinigchinich," written by Father Geronimo Boscana, a missionary at San Juan Capistrano from 1814 to 1826. Chinigchinich, a man born in a Gabrielino village in present-day Long Beach, established himself as the successor

Local traders and merchants often stopped to converse and barter with the Spanish missionaries, as depicted in this early illustration by C.R. Couch. Courtesy, Anaheim Public Library

to Wiyot and created a new social order for the Juaneños.

In the center of the villages, a fenced-off ceremonial plaza was cleared, containing an inner chamber called a *vanquech*. Inside, Chinigchinich was represented with a feather-filled coyote skin, deer horns, the claws of a mountain lion, beaks of hawks, and the talons of crows. Protruding from the mouth were arrow shafts, adding ferocity to the image.

Few were allowed to see the figure. The village council, known as the *puplem*, were the only ones, and only for special occasions, such as tribal feast days and days reserved for adoration of Chinigchinich.

The vanquech was so sacred, it could be used as a sanctuary by criminals. If he could reach it in time, a murderer, thief, or adulterer could go free. Still, the crime could be avenged, and often was upon another member of the family.

Anthropologists believe Chinigchinich lived relatively recently, and that he was influenced by Christianity. Though local Indians never saw Spaniards until 1769, word of the conquest of Mexico in the sixteenth century probably reached the area through the vast trade routes that stretched across the continent. The basics of Christianity were probably included in the news, and Chinigchinich may have incorporated them in his new social order. There are definite resemblances to Christianity that don't match up well with traditional Indian ideas. Chinigchinich presented himself as a god-like creature and threatened punishment to all who opposed him—often by sending black wid-

ows, scorpions, and rattlesnakes—thus going against the grain of traditional Indian thought. At the peak of his influence, he issued his commands from Santa Catalina Island. Near the end of his life, he returned to Long Beach, where his followers said he died and ascended to the equivalent of heaven.

Chinigchinich was a Gabrielino, but there is little evidence that his cult spread widely among his own people. Gabrielino mythology traces time back to a creator called Kwawar, who set the earth upon the shoulders of seven giants. Earthquakes were caused by their stirrings. As in many Indian religions, animals played key roles. Porpoises circled the world, making sure everything was in good order. Crows warned of the approach of strangers.

Even if Gabrielinos did not follow Chinigchinich, both the Gabrielinos and Juaneños tribes shared much of the same culture and lifestyle. An example were the jimson weed ceremonies, in which members took a drug mixture thought to offer strength and protection. At puberty, a boy underwent a ceremony designed to measure his toughness and fitness to join the men of the tribe. He was branded on the upper arm, whipped with nettles, and laid on ant hills. A girl did not have it much easier; she lay on a bed of heated stones, fasting for days while women sang and danced around her.

Wives were purchased for marriage, and husbands were free to punish them for infidelity—even with death. Usually the husband would simply trade wives with the seducer.

Indian homes were made of a framework of poles thatched with vegetation. Each village had its chief, whose title was passed upon death to the eldest son.

Generally, the Juaneños and Gabrielinos of the Anaheim area lived a peaceful life, in harmony with a bountiful land. But the peace would not last. The white man was at hand.

Missions and Ranchos

Spanish exploration had touched upon the California coast as early as 1542. But it wasn't until more than two centuries later that the first land expedition was ordered. Gaspar de Portola arrived in San Diego in mid-1769 with 62 men, ready to make the long trek to Monterey Bay, where they were to meet a sea expedition also leaving from San Diego.

Portola's main purpose was to make a firm claim on Alta California, heading off Russian threats to explore the area. Later a system of missions was established to teach Christian ways to the native Indians.

The journey began on July 16, 1769. Already exhausted by a long sea voyage, Portola's men now had to contend with unfamiliar terrain and unknown obstacles. Marches were short, ending early in the day so scouts could check the next day's terrain and look for water.

Portola's men became the first Europeans to travel through today's Orange County. The Indians, meeting white men for the first time, were friendly to the travellers. Two young Indian girls were baptized near San Clemente in an area that was named Cristianitos Canyon. A few days later, Portola's expedition camped on the Santa Ana River—just over the border from present-day Anaheim—and were greeted by members of an Indian village. The Indians gave the soldiers gifts and invited the newcomers to live with them. Later the Spaniards crossed the river and made their way north.

Portola passed Monterey without realizing it, missed the sea expedition, and ended up in San Francisco. The soldiers retraced their steps in a painful trek back to San Diego. But they had paved the way for the mission priests to follow.

Established in 1771, the Mission San Gabriel was the fourth mission to be founded by Father Junipero Serra. Artist Ferdinand Deppe provided a rare glimpse into mission life in this 1832 painting, capturing the time when the light of the mission burned the brightest. Courtesy, Santa Barbara Mission Archives

With lands comprising most of southern Orange County, Mission San Juan Capistrano was the seventh mission to be founded under the California mission system. Pictured here in 1938, the mission has undergone several attempted renovations over the years, and is still undergoing restorations today. Courtesy, Anaheim Public Library

The missions, under the leadership of Father Junipero Serra, were founded one by one. The fourth, Mission San Gabriel, was established in 1771, and controlled much of Los Angeles and all of Orange County north of the Santa Ana River. The seventh, Mission San Juan Capistrano, was founded in 1776 and took in south Orange County.

The decision whether to convert was left to the Indian, at least ostensibly, but once a choice was made, it was for good. The Indian was given room and board, but in return he gave his life to the mission. If he ran away, he was brought back and punished. He also gave up virtually all of his Indian culture, though the Spaniards tolerated native games and dances.

How well the Indians were treated is still a matter of controversy. While there is no historical evidence that Spaniards mistreated them, Juaneño tradition contends that there were beatings and whippings. The fact that mission listings are disproportionately filled with the names of women and children suggests that men stayed away and that relations were not entirely amicable.

The missions were given 10 years to teach the Indians Western ways and prepare them for land ownership. Thousands of acres were to be held in trust for the Indians. For whatever reason, the process took more than half a century and ended only when mission control was taken away by the new people in charge—the Mexican government.

After a long struggle, Mexico won its independence from Spain in 1821 and then instituted a series of acts that gradually removed power from the missions. The new Mexican Constitution freed the Indians. But the Indians were not prepared for their sudden release; some left for the hills and their old culture, while others took work on the ranchos that were taking over mission lands. The missions declined and fell into disrepair.

The first ranchos began as Spanish land grants, but it wasn't until after Mexican independence that Alta California became a puzzle-like patchwork of ranchos. Would-be landowners applied to the governor, supplying personal information, a description of the land, and a *diseno,* or map. The petition was referred to a local official, who investigated and then sent the governor an *informe*, or report. If favorable, the governor issued the grant.

Rancho boundaries were based on geographical features rather than fences, so cattle could roam the land. Surveys were made by horsemen who used a rope tied to two stakes to determine the ranch boundaries. Steer skulls and slashes on trees were typical markers. Nothing more was necessary. Land was too cheap and plentiful to worry about precision.

The "Days of the Dons" were a romantic time. Rodeos were festive occasions; visitors came for fine meals, dance, and drink. Horse racing was the most popular sport, but men also indulged in *corrida de toros*. In this sport a bull was lassoed by the horns and dragged into an arena where the beast was baited with serapes and a sharp lance. He was then driven out the gate by the horsemen. The swiftest grabbed the bull's tail and threw him down, a feat called "tailing the bull."

The ranchos did a brisk business trading the hides and tallow from their cattle. The slender Spanish cattle were not bred for their meat, which was too difficult to ship to outside markets.

One of the larger ranchos of Southern California was San Juan Cajon de Santa Ana, within whose boundaries would emerge not only Anaheim, but also Fullerton, Placentia, and Brea. Patricio Ontiveros, a former official on the nearby Los Nietos grant, applied for the land in 1833. But he died before his application could be approved, and it was granted to his son, Juan Pacifico, on May 13, 1837.

The total grant was a little under

LEFT: Franciscan missionary Junipero Serra founded nine of the great California missions during his years of devout and tireless work for the church. Courtesy, Bancroft Library

The rancheros of Southern California prospered during the early 1800s when demand for cattle was high and land holdings were spread far and wide. Courtesy, Historical Collection, First American Title Insurance Company

Rodeos, horse races, and bullfights were among some of the favorite recreational activities during the golden years of the rancheros. This Vischer print depicts a spring rodeo scene on an early California rancho. Courtesy, California Section, California State Library

36,000 acres and covered with mustard grass, chaparral, and cactus. Snakes, rabbits, coyotes, ground squirrels, gophers, and insects made their home on the land, still largely untouched by man.

Juan Pacifico Ontiveros and his wife, Martina, dreamed of a simple, prosperous life on the rancho, and it appears they enjoyed one. In addition to cattle, he raised barley and other crops. Irrigation ditches from the Santa Ana River ran to his house and an area called "Ontiveros' Garden." Indians did most of the work.

His oldest daughter, Petra, married August Langenberger, a young German, who later became Anaheim's first merchant.

But the Ontiveros' idyllic lifestyle did not last forever. The Mexican War, and subsequent victory by the United States, signalled big changes for California, not the least for the ranchos. In the Treaty of Guadalupe Hildalgo, signed in 1848, Mexico ceded all of her lands north of the Rio Grande, from Texas to the Pacific Ocean, to the United States. Two years later California became the 31st state.

The treaty guaranteed the property

rights of Mexican citizens, but only as long as they could prove they owned the land. Every ranchero had to submit claims to a three-member land commission set up by the U.S. Congress. This proved disastrous to many rancheros; the imprecise geographical boundaries and lax record-keeping simply would not do under the U.S. system. Many lost their land, and those lucky enough to win their claims did so only after costly, time-consuming legal battles. Some gave their land to Americans promising to eliminate their debt in exchange. Others fought a losing fight against squatters, who decided to bypass the legalities and settle where they wanted.

Ontiveros was one of many rancheros who found the claim system an endless legal maze. He had lost some of the papers proving his ownership during a boundary dispute several years before. Witnesses attested to his ownership, but his claim was rejected.

Not to be denied, Ontiveros hired the best attorney in the field, Jonathan R. Scott, and appealed. George Hansen, deputy surveyor of Los Angeles County, resur-

veyed the land. After exhaustive testimony, Ontiveros was awarded his claim on January 29, 1856. An appeal by the government was rejected the next year. Still, it wasn't until 1877—nearly a quarter century after Ontiveros filed his claim—that President Rutherford Hayes signed the document, formally approving the claim.

Long before the dispute was settled, Ontiveros decided to leave the rancho and move to a new one in Santa Maria. In 1857, he heard from the young surveyor Hansen and a young musician/vintner from San Francisco named John Frohling. They were interested in buying a portion of his rancho. A new dream was about to begin.

Madame Modjeska and the Polish Colony

Adding a slightly different flavor to the now thriving community of Anaheim was the brief influence of a small colony of Polish

artists who arrived in 1876. The group included Madame Helena Modjeska, already famous for her acting. Another member, Henryk Sienkiewicz, would later write the Nobel Prize-winning novel *Quo Vadis?*

The group was seeking greater freedom than they had living in Russian-ruled Poland. Karol Bozenta Chlapowski, Modjeska's husband, had heard of Anaheim and sent Sienkiewicz and another friend to the colony to investigate the possibility of relocating there. Both were delighted with the area.

Modjeska recently had suffered a physical collapse from the stress of being closely watched by Russian authorities and the sudden loss of both her brother and her best friend. She and the others saw rustic Anaheim as a place where she could start a new life as a farmer. The group rented a small house on West Center Street and set about creating a utopian art

RIGHT: German native August Langenberger first immigrated to New Orleans before coming to Anaheim via Northern California. In 1856, he married Petra Ontiveros, the daughter of Juan Pacifico Ontiveros, who was the owner of the Rancho San Juan Cajon de Santa Ana. Langenberger went on to establish Anaheim's first permanent store in an adobe building on Center Street. Courtesy, Anaheim Public Library

colony that lived off the land. "What wild dreams we dreamt!" she later wrote. "What visions of freedom, peace, and happiness flitted across our brains! . . . I pictured to myself a life of toil under the blue skies of California, among the hills, riding on horseback with a gun over my shoulder. I imagined all sorts of things except what really was in store for me."

What was in store were the harsh realities of farm life, a world without servants to cook or clean house. She tried cooking without good results.

Other members of the colony didn't take to the new life any better. The men, with hands used to artistic endeavors, found farm work exhausting and backbreaking. After only a few months, the colony broke up. Chlapowski spent more than $15,000 trying to make the venture work,

and toward the end Modjeska was forced to pawn some of her furs to save money.

She decided to learn English and return to the stage. She did so in grand fashion, going on to become a leading lady of the American stage. She travelled around the country, returning occasionally to rest at her new home in the Santa Ana Mountains in the canyon that today is named for her. She called her rustic home Arden, after the Forest of Arden in Shakespeare's *As You Like It*. Modjeska never again lived in the German colony that gave her a bitter taste of the farming life. She finished her life in a new home in Newport Beach, where she died in 1908. Anaheim has honored her with a statue that stands in Pearson Park, as she appeared in her favorite role: Mary, Queen of Scots.

August Langenberger's two-story adobe, shown here in 1858, served as residence, general store, bank, and as an office for the Wells Fargo Express Company. Located on Center Street, the adobe was a hub of activity in early Anaheim and was the principal trading center between Mission San Gabriel and Mission San Juan Capistrano. Courtesy, Anaheim Public Library

Madame Helena Modjeska came to Anaheim in 1876 to help establish a Polish artists' colony with her family and friends. After an unsuccessful attempt at farming, Modjeska went to San Francisco to learn English, so that she could pursue her talents as an actress on the American stage. With her Shakespearean training and past European success, Modjeska's celebrated stage career in the United States spanned a period of more than 20 years. Modjeska's love and admiration for the Anaheim area did not wane throughout her travels. She had a canyon home built in the beautiful Santa Ana Mountains and lived there for many years. Modjeska eventually retired to Bay Island in Newport Beach where she lived out her remaining years. Courtesy, Anaheim Public Library

William Koenig was superintendent for John Frohling and Charles Kohler at the 20-acre vineyard they had established in Los Angeles shortly before the Anaheim venture. Koenig moved to the Mother Colony in 1869 and started his own viticulture business. He was often referred to as the "boss of the cellar," because of his winemaking experience and success. Koenig's vineyard, wine cellar, and residence are depicted in this late 1800s illustration. Courtesy, Anaheim Public Library

Campo Aleman

The land that John Frohling and George Hansen wanted for their wine colony was not much to look at; it was covered by scrub, cactus, and chaparral, and home only to jackrabbits and rattlesnakes. The landowner, Juan Pacifico Ontiveros, candidly told the would-be purchasers that the land "couldn't support a goat." And truthfully, the land wasn't the first choice of the two newcomers.

But Hansen had recently resurveyed it for the ranchero's claim, and he knew which part of it he wanted to get and how to make it better. All that was needed was water, and that would soon be flowing from the nearby Santa Ana River.

Frohling and his business partner up north, Charles Kohler, had chosen Hansen to be the superintendent of a dream: To create out of this treeless wasteland of brush and jackrabbits one of the most productive vineyards in the world, which would be tended by a group of 50 Germans.

Born in Prussia in 1827, Frohling had taken flute lessons at an early age. But restlessness drove him to America. Arriving in New York in 1843 at the age of 16, he gradually made his way west until he ended up in San Francisco 10 years later. There he met Charles Kohler, a violinist, and they became part of a string band called the Verandah Concert Society.

But the two had more than music on their minds. Relaxing one day at a picnic, they decided they wanted to go into the wine business.

The choice was certainly not based on a whim. By the early 1850s, the raising of grapes was already a major industry in California, second only to cattle raising, and it was growing rapidly. In 1855, there was a total of 324,000 vines in the state, a figure that rose to 1.5 million in 1856. By 1859, there were 6.5 million vines.

Working out of an office in San Francisco, the two musicians soon had a profitable business. But they sought a more steady source of grapes and bought a 20-acre vineyard in the Los Angeles area. Frohling left to manage the Los Angeles vineyard while Kohler tended to business up north.

The 20-acre vineyard was not enough to meet the growing needs of the firm, which was still forced to buy grapes from other vineyards. So Kohler and Frohling began planning for something bigger, a colony wholly devoted to viniculture.

The proposed colony was to be composed entirely of Germans; there were many in the San Francisco area. Most had fled their homeland during the revolution of 1848, as others fought the tyranny of Frederick William IV of Prussia. Many settled in San Francisco, a wild and often violent western town. Some of the German families wanted a more peaceful place to settle and the wine colony proposal was very appealing.

George Hansen was recommended to Frohling as a man with talents well suited to the venture. Born in Austria in 1824, Hansen came to California in 1850 in search of gold. Finding little, he left for Los Angeles in 1853 and soon became deputy surveyor. Hansen understood the engineering problems behind the winery project. That he was fluent in both German and English was another plus.

In early 1857, Hansen drafted the bylaws for what became the Los Angeles

George Hansen was a key individual in making the community of Anaheim a reality. He drew up bylaws for the proposed colony and was appointed superintendent. Hansen was also responsible for acquiring the land from Juan Pacifico Ontiveros on which Anaheim was later built. Courtesy, Anaheim Public Library

Vineyard Society. A few days after the bylaws were adopted, 23 people subscribed for 27 memberships at $250 apiece. On March 2, 1857, Hansen was unanimously chosen superintendent of the project, with a salary of $200 per month for the first three years. Fifty dollars of each month's salary was to be withheld until the project's completion.

Hansen's first task was to find a suitable site. Although he was familiar with Rancho San Juan Cajon de Santa Ana and knew Ontiveros, it was not his first choice. He feared that the flow from the Santa Ana River would not be reliable and preferred land that could be irrigated by the San Gabriel River.

He tried to buy land from two other ranchos close to the San Gabriel, but neither effort succeeded. Kohler was dispatched by the society's impatient board of directors to "try and hurry along the selection" of a site.

Meanwhile, Hansen finally approached Ontiveros. Even if his rancho wasn't Hansen's first choice, he decided it could work, and recommended the land to Frohling and the society board. They agreed, and the purchase was made: 1,165 acres of land, carefully selected by Hansen, at two dollars an acre. Ontiveros did not own the land where the irrigation canal would have to be dug, so an easement to the Santa Ana River was purchased from the man who did, Bernardo Yorba.

Most of Hansen's work still lay ahead of him. The land now had to be cleared of brush and a five-mile ditch had to be dug from the Santa Ana River. Branches of the ditch were dug to all parts of the colony-to-be, bringing the total to fifteen miles. A living fence of willow trees was planted around the perimeter in an effort to keep cattle from wandering onto the vineyards. Eight-foot poles were placed a foot and a half apart, with more willow poles attached with tarred rope yarn.

Hansen, of course, did not do all the work himself. About a hundred laborers were used, including Indians, Mexicans, Spaniards, and others.

The surveyor put his engineering skills to good use. He had the ditch dug along a ridge that tilted slightly to the southwest, and made the colony's north and south boundary run parallel to the ridge. The ridge today is marked by Sycamore Street.

The colony-to-be needed a name. The society met on January 15, 1858, and voted on three suggestions: Annaheim, Annagau, and Weinheim. The first vote was close—Annaheim, 18; Annagau, 17; Weinheim, 1. Since there was no majority, another vote was held. This time the result was Annaheim, 20, and Annagau, 18. The society had agreed upon a name. Some time afterward, the extra "n" was dropped by general consent.

The name was derived from the German word "heim," meaning home, and the Spanish "Ana," referring to the Santa Ana River.

In its January 30 edition, the *Los Angeles Star* ran a lengthy report on the colony's progress and praised the name as "not only euphonious, but expressive. It is suggestive of the most pleasing associations, reminding one of the wide-spreading

and lightly cultivated vineyards of the Fatherland."

The townsite was laid out with 64 building lots placed in the center of a site; each lot was about a half-acre in size. Later, 50 of the lots were distributed to society members, with the remaining 14 reserved for public use. Twenty-acre parcels from the surrounding land were given to each vintner.

The townsite was bounded by North, East, South, and West streets, which today still accurately mark the boundary of the original colony. Four gates were installed at each end of Los Angeles Street (now Anaheim Boulevard) and Center Street (now Lincoln Avenue). At the south was the San Diego Gate, to the west the San

Pedro Gate, to the north the Los Angeles Gate, and to the east the Santa Ana River Gate, each named for its destination. Hitching posts were installed both inside and outside the gates, so a rider could tie his horse while he opened and closed the gate.

One of the many crucial decisions that Hansen had to make in the beginning was the type of grape to grow. He settled upon the Mission variety (now called the Criolla), which had been developed in Mexico and brought to California by the Franciscan fathers of the missions for use in sacraments and for table wine. The grape's most obvious advantage was that three-fourths of the grapes then grown in the state were Mission grapes,

Many viticulture enterprises developed in Anaheim's early years, creating new jobs and skills for the area's hardy colonists. These three vintners are shown bottling wine for the Ernest Browning Winery in the late 1800s. Courtesy, Anaheim Public Library

RIGHT: Built by George Hansen as his home and office, the Mother Colony House is a symbol of Anaheim's heritage. After going through several owners, the house was obtained by the Mother Colony chapter of the Daughters of the American Revolution. Opened in 1929, it is now the oldest museum in Orange County, with many pieces on display, including a blue and white toiletry set that was a wedding gift to Clementine Schmidt and August Langenberger. Courtesy, Anaheim Public Library

RIGHT: Built by George Hansen as his home and office, the Mother Colony House is a symbol of Anaheim's heritage. After going through several owners, the house was obtained by the Mother Colony chapter of the Daughters of the American Revolution. Opened in 1929, it is now the oldest museum in Orange County, with many pieces on display, including a blue and white toiletry set that was a wedding gift to Clementine Schmidt and August Langenberger. Courtesy, Anaheim Public Library

BELOW: The Anaheim Water Company was founded in 1859 to sell and supply water to the newly established community, and in 1884 was renamed the Anaheim Union Water Company. Pictured here is a group of company employees, circa 1940. Courtesy, Anaheim Public Library

and there would be no difficulty in buying an adequate supply at a low price. There was no desire to experiment with any of several foreign varieties, whose mettle in Southern California's climate was only then being tested.

The Mission grape did have drawbacks. It was considered good mainly for white dessert wines, and judged to make a poor port or sherry because of its lack of color and acid. Another disadvantage—not to be discovered until much later—was its susceptibility to certain diseases.

The choice was made, and laborers planted 400,000 vines. In addition to the Mission grape, a mix of others was planted, including Barcelona, Malviosic, Zinfandel, and Mataro.

As the work progressed, a series of assessments were levied on each of the shareholders, making the total investment per share $1,280.

A New Community

The land had been readied and the vines had been planted. Now all that was needed were the families to raise the grapes. The first to arrive from San Francisco in Sep-

tember 1859, the Hammes and the Rehms, landed in San Pedro before making the long ride to Anaheim.

Only a few buildings had been erected for the new community. The first was Hansen's home and office, built at the northeast corner of today's Lincoln Avenue and Anaheim Boulevard. In the 1920s, the house was moved to its present site on West Street, and today it is preserved as a city museum and known as the Mother Colony House.

The newcomers were a diverse lot. They included watchmakers, carpenters, a cooper, a blacksmith, a dry goods merchant, a carriage maker, a cabinet maker, and a brewer. None of them were vintners. But they would soon learn.

As the new residents began to trickle in, the Anaheim Water Company was created in 1859 to sell and supply water in the community. It also took over all the assets of the Los Angeles Vineyard Society. The latter closed its books, its purpose completed.

The new colonists went to work. In late 1861, the *Star* reported that 75,000 gal-

lons of "very superior quality" wine had been made at the settlement. But it was not going to be that easy for the vintners who were still learning. Several years of freakish weather quickly hampered their efforts, starting with a rainstorm that commenced on December 24, 1861, and persisted nearly unbroken for four weeks. The normally tame Santa Ana River leaped its banks and left a sheet of water from the Santa Ana Mountains to the Coyote Hills miles away. The flood washed out several of Anaheim's adobes and drowned Frederick Goetz, one of the original settlers, while he was doing rescue work.

The flood receded, only to be replaced by severe drought in both 1863 and 1864. The dryness took a terrible toll on the thousands of cattle that still roamed much of the surrounding area. What was once lush grazing land was soon littered with the carcasses of thousands of cattle.

Anaheim's willow fence was no longer enough to keep out the starving and thirsty beasts, drawn to the irrigated vineyards. *Vaqueros* were hired to shoot them as they approached. The Anaheim Wa-

Benjamin Dreyfus built this large winery in the mid-1880s, as Anaheim's vineyards prospered. The main building measured 80 feet by 200 feet. Unfortunately, neither Dreyfus nor the area's vintner industry would survive long enough to help it succeed. Dreyfus died in early 1886 at a time when an insidious blight was starting its total destruction of the Anaheim vineyards. Although this facility was a winery for only a brief amount of time, it was used for a variety of purposes over the years until it was eventually torn down in 1973. Courtesy, Anaheim Public Library

ABOVE: Frederick W. Kuelp came to Anaheim as the community's first schoolmaster in the early 1860s. Urged to move to the area from San Francisco, Kuelp and his wife hesitated at first due to financial circumstances. The colonists finally agreed to help with the relocation by furnishing Kuelp and his wife with living quarters and some food. Kuelp was also able to obtain extra fees as Anaheim's justice of the peace and as a notary public. Courtesy, Anaheim Public Library

ter Company voted to have vintners plant a strip of cactus around the colony. But some residents refused to cooperate, so the shooting continued. In the end, it was more humane than the cactus, which would have simply turned the cattle away to starve. The drought brought an abrupt end to California's cattle industry and hastened the end of the ranchos, which were increasingly being taken over by American farmers.

The drought drastically cut the flow from the Santa Ana River. The Anaheim Water Company dug a new ditch farther up the river. Irrigation water was restricted to the older vines.

When the vintners weren't coaxing their vines through severe drought, they endured grasshoppers, which periodically descended upon their fields in incessant waves.

Despite hard times, the dream of a prosperous colony was slowly coming to pass. Production from the original planting of 400,000 vines grew each year, rising from 75,000 gallons in 1861 to 300,000 gallons three years later.

Although Anaheim was a colony with a single purpose, each vintner was essentially on his own. This scattered approach worked reasonably well at first, but some growers yearned for a more efficient way of marketing the town's grapes. The result was the United Anaheim Wine Growers' Association, formed in 1863. The partnership enabled vintners to promote and sell their grapes together. The manager, Benjamin Dreyfus, moved to San Francisco—then still the business center of the West Coast—to set up an office. Later, the association set up another office in New York.

The colonists decided the only port close to them, Wilmington, was too expensive. A group of vintners searched the coastline and selected the closer site of Alamitos Bay. The water was too shallow for oceangoing ships, so two lighters were built to cover the distance between the ships and the pier. The Anaheim Lighter Company was formed in 1864 by a group made up mostly of Anaheim colonists. The two lighters were moved by pulling a cable that extended from the pier to a buoy 500 feet offshore. Loaded freight wagons made frequent trips between the port and the colony. The going was rough in winter, when much of the land in between turned to marsh.

An 1867 flood changed the course of the San Gabriel River and spilled tons of silt into Alamitos Bay, suddenly rendering the dock facilities useless. The lighter company obtained a 20-year lease from the state to create a new port at Bolsa Chiquita, about a mile and a half south. The new port, known as Anaheim Landing, served the area for many years and later became a popular vacation spot. Today, it is known as Anaheim Bay, inside the U.S. Naval Weapons Station

at Seal Beach.

Just as the new colony's name was a mixture of German and Spanish, so was its lifestyle. Though all of the new colonists were German, they were heavily influenced by nearby Mexican residents, who called the new town "Campo Aleman," or German camp. The colony was sometimes a polyglot of languages, with many residents speaking either German, English, or Spanish, the choice depending on the circumstances.

Anaheim had a distinct German flavor, but not wholly as German as its population makeup might indicate. As one early investor, John Hittell, put it:

Anaheim will never have the foreign character which marks many German villages in the valley states of the Mississippi, where the English language is not known to any of the people. All of the Anaheimers have lived for sometime elsewhere in the United States . . . The English language will be the predominant tongue, although German will long be cherished.

Still, until 1871, all of the minutes of the Anaheim Water Company were written in German.

A Place to Learn, Worship, and Work

At first the new community had well-educated citizens, but no schools or teachers. One of the lot owners, Frederick W. Kuelp, was a teacher, but he remained in San Francisco to teach at his private school. He had been hit hard by the lot assessments and insisted that he did not have enough money to build a dwelling on his lot.

Finally colonists persuaded Kuelp to move, offering his family living quarters and other assistance. The first school was set up in an old Indian adobe lodging house, a structure built earlier to house unmarried Indian laborers. Kuelp had nine pupils his first year, four of them from the nearby community of Olive.

Residents kept the Kuelps stocked in fruits and vegetables, and he added to his teaching income with fees from serving as the town's justice of the peace and a notary public. Later a new adobe was built on Anaheim Water Company property, becoming both a school and living quarters for the Kuelps. But the adobe collapsed in the flood of 1862, also destroying the piano on which Mrs. Kuelp earned extra money through piano lessons. The school was eventually moved back into the Indian lodging house.

Growth resulted in the formation of the Anaheim School District in 1867, giving the community more control over its educational system. But the growth only added to the overwork and bad health that plagued Kuelp. Finally, he collapsed in 1869 and died two years later.

The school board found an able replacement in a young Civil War veteran and Oberlin graduate who had come west for his health, James M. Guinn. Guin soon expanded the school year from seven months to nine and oversaw the building of a new one-room schoolhouse. Starting in 1871, all school examinations were done orally, with parents and others invited to attend. The first high school classes were added in 1874.

Soon a new school was needed, and

LEFT: James M. Guinn began teaching in Anaheim after the death of his predecessor Frederick W. Kuelp in 1869. Guinn soon realized the necessity of improving the educational system, but found there was no mor.zy to build a much needed new schoolhouse. In 1876 he successfully introduced a bill to the state legislature calling for the construction of new school facilities through a bond issue. Guinn's success represented the first schoolhouse built in California through a bond issue. Courtesy, Anaheim Public Library

FACING PAGE, BOTTOM: Henryk Sienkiewicz, pictured here, and Jules Sypniewski arrived from Poland in 1876 to locate a place in which to establish an artists' colony for their followers, a group that included the famous Polish actress, Madame Helena Modjeska. Sypniewski returned to Poland with a favorable report, while Sienkiewicz stayed behind to observe and to write about the area and its people. It was reported that Sienkiewicz spent many hours at Anaheim Landing collecting his material, as well as relaxing in its tranquil environment. Courtesy, Anaheim Public Library

These Anaheim first-graders pose for a class portrait with their teacher on the steps of their school in 1898. Courtesy, Anaheim Public Library

in 1876, Guinn suggested the novel idea of financing it through bonds. He drafted state legislation to fund the new building through a $10,000 bond issue. It passed, and the two-story building, Central School, opened for classes on January 16, 1879—the first school in California built through a bond issue. Guinn introduced other innovations before he left Anaheim to become superintendent of Los Angeles schools in 1881, including the division of students into grades and the first written examinations in the state.

One institution conspicuous by its absence in the early years was a church. Despite some claims since then that the colony was full of antireligious "free-thinkers" who passed a law prohibiting churches, the truth was simply that protestant ministers were scarce at the time in Southern California, particularly German-speaking Lutherans.

The omission was finally corrected in the late 1860s with the building of St. Boniface Catholic Church on a lot donated by

the Anaheim Water Company. A hastily built structure, described as a "little larger than an ordinary sitting room," was torn down in 1879 and replaced with a larger building.

A petition by 24 residents of the area in 1870 prompted the formation of the city's first Presbyterian church, with the Reverend Lemuel P. Webber as its first pastor. Three years later, a wooden church was built in Anaheim for about $3,000.

Webber dreamed of a new colony made wholly of Presbyterians, and in 1871 founded the new town of Westminster, located seven miles to the southwest. The temperance colony forbid "manufacturing, buying or selling intoxicating beverages except for sanitary or scientific purposes," a dictum obeyed until Westminster's first saloon opened in 1890. Webber did not live to see the new colony prosper. While continuing to serve the Anaheim church, he was soaked by a heavy rain while driving back from a prayer meeting. He became ill and died in 1874 at 42.

The first Episcopal church was founded in 1873 through the efforts of Susan and Elizabeth Lafaucherie. The sisters started an Episcopal Sunday school and petitioned to have the San Gabriel minister include Anaheim in his circuit. Soon the growing congregation acquired a more permanent minister, and St. Michael's Episcopal Church was built in 1876 on Adele and Emily streets.

Other social organizations emerged. The Masons organized a lodge in 1870, and the Odd Fellows followed with their own lodge two years later.

The town's first merchants were Benjamin Dreyfus and August Langenberger, who established a general store in a two-story adobe building on Lincoln Avenue by 1859 before the first vintners arrived. In addition to selling general merchandise, the building served as a hotel, dining room, bar, and residence for the Langenberger family.

Langenberger was a German native who joined the 1849 gold rush, then came south to marry Ontiveros' daughter Petra. He played a major role as the colony developed, becoming the agent for the Wells, Fargo & Company stage line that soon served Anaheim and later serving on the city council, school board, and county board of supervisors. Dreyfus, who furnished the capital for the store, became one of the colony's most productive vintners. Their store was a fixture in Anaheim in its early years.

The colony's first hotel was the Anaheim Hotel, opened in 1867 by its proprietress, Pauline Van Gulpen. The "pretentious combined frame and adobe building," as one person described it, also became a place for grand balls and occasional Saturday night dances. A second place for visitors, a two-story wooden structure called the Planter's Hotel, was opened the next year by the town's first postmaster, John Fischer. The Planter's burned down in 1871 in a furious blaze

that sent embers flying to nearby buildings, which were saved only by heroic efforts. Undaunted, Fischer quickly built a new hotel on the same site. In 1890, under a different owner, the Planter's burned down again. This time it wasn't rebuilt.

Visitors to the prosperous community were often impressed. One, Brigadier General James F. Rusling, who stopped by in 1867 later wrote, "We drove through the clean and well-kept streets, scenting Rhineland on every side; and indeed, this Anaheim itself is nothing but a bit of Germany dropped down on the Pacific Coast."

As time went on, Anaheim attracted notice in travel books and other publications. A frequent theme of such

ABOVE: Constructed on a plot of land donated by the Anaheim Water Company in the late 1860s, St. Boniface Catholic Church was named for the English missionary and archbishop who founded the great Benedictine Monastery of Fulda. The first church structure was later replaced with a larger building in 1879. Courtesy, Anaheim Public Library

ABOVE, LEFT: The First Presbyterian Church of Anaheim realized its beginnings in 1870, when a request to organize a church was called to order. It was at this parish that the Reverend Lemuel P. Webber, who later founded the community of Westminster, maintained his ministerial obligations. Courtesy, Anaheim Public Library

RIGHT: When John F.
Fischer opened the Plant-
er's Hotel in 1868, it was
referred to as a "commo-
dious" and important
hostelry. In June 1871,
however, the hotel fell
victim to a devastating
fire that reduced it to
ashes. But due to Fischer's
determined attitude, it
reopened later that year
in November. Courtesy,
Anaheim Public Library

BELOW: Less than 20
years after August Langenberger and Benjamin
Dreyfus established their
general store in a two-
story adobe in 1858, their
mercantile business had developed to the point
where they needed to con-
struct new facilities. This
structure was erected in
1874 to serve the growing
needs of Anaheim's expanding population. Courtesy,
Historical Collection,
First American Title Insurance Company

writings was the image of the town as a health resort. Charles Nordhoff's 1873 book *California for Health, Pleasure and Residence* included an entire chapter on the city, plus a long testimonial letter from Francis S. Miles, a consumptive, claiming to find the relief that all the renowned spas of Europe couldn't provide. In *Semi-Tropical California*, Ben C. Truman wrote of Anaheim that "nowhere else in the world can be found atmospheric and climatic conditions so favorable to those suffering from pulmonary affections."

A sanitorium was built on South Lemon Street in 1876 by Dr. James Ellis, an Englishman who claimed that the area's climate was superior to famous Mediterranean resorts "for relief of asthma and catarrhal and inflammatory phthisis."

Anaheim's vintners did nothing to dispel such claims. An 1869 brochure advertising the products of the Anaheim Wine Growers' Association not only reinforced the idea, but disputed any notion that residents of the vintner colony ever got tipsy: "Intoxication is unknown . . . yet all partake of the pure wine which 'maketh glad the heart of man.' The absence of doctors in Anaheim was no problem," it continued, "as the place is perfectly healthy, and during the existence of the settlement they have had no

deaths and but little illness."

Of course, it was all too good to be true. Consumption, diphtheria, and other diseases were problems in a town with no hospitals. The town did have doctors, who made their rounds on horseback.

In early Anaheim, families lit their homes with kerosene lamps, drew their household water in buckets from wells, and warmed themselves with wood stoves.

Anaheim's dirt streets were either sprinkled occasionally to keep down the dust or covered with straw. The straw provided a home for fleas and occasionally

caught fire.

Wines were not the only libations the community had to offer. Beer was a necessity to the many vintners who longed for anything but wine after a long day in the fields. At first, it came from elsewhere, but the colony's first brewery began operation in 1870, and was followed within a few years by a second.

Outings sometimes found residents among the ancient oak trees of what is today Irvine Regional Park, but then known simply as the "Picnic Grounds."

Change in the Air

But Anaheim was undergoing major changes. By 1870 the town had a population of about 800 and was the second largest community in Los Angeles County. Residents were feeling the inconvenience of traveling along terrible roads during the day's journey that was required to reach the county seat. They also resented that most of their tax dollars were going to projects in the northern part of the county.

To win more clout, the town incorporated in 1870. Led by Mayor Max Strobel, residents campaigned to create a new County of Anaheim from the southeastern corner of Los Angeles County. A bill was introduced in the state assembly and was passed before L.A. politicians realized what had happened. L.A. politicians united, and through a determined effort defeated the bill in the Senate, ending the first of what would be seven attempts to split from Los Angeles.

The colorful Strobel had a brief, but profound, impact on the city. A man of ad-

venture, he had come west with John C. Frémont and participated in an insurrection in Nicaragua that later turned sour. In addition to the incorporation effort, Strobel formed the Anaheim Railway Company, which was supposed to connect the city with Anaheim Landing through a narrow-gauge railway that would extend eventually to San Bernardino. But the plan went nowhere, and Strobel died in 1873 while in London, where he was acting as an agent for a proposed sale of Santa Catalina Island.

Local merchants soon saw the need for a newspaper, and in 1870 offered to subsidize anyone who could start one. Attorney George Washington Barter, who previously helped to publish the *Los Angeles Star*, responded to the offer. Barter acquired an old hand-press from the defunct *Wilmington Journal* and published the first issue of the *Anaheim Gazette* on October 29, 1870. It was not only Anaheim's first newspaper, but the first in what would become Orange County.

The feisty Barter helped to launch numerous campaigns, including a second secession effort. His controversial stands sometimes angered their intended targets, in one case prompting a fist fight that Barter won handily. But the flamboyant editor's tenure was brief. After buying the *Los Angeles Star*, Barter sold the *Gazette* in October 1871 to Charles A. Gardner. The name was changed to the *Southern Californian*, but the old name of *Gazette* was restored in 1875.

Other changes were brewing. In the early years, Anaheim's great distance from other towns—the closest town of

Founder of the Planter's Hotel and secretary of the Los Angeles Vineyard Society, John F. Fischer was one of the prominent citizens who helped develop Anaheim into a prosperous business community. Shown here in the late 1800s, Fischer also served as Anaheim's first postmaster. Courtesy, Anaheim Public Library

any size was Los Angeles—enforced a kind of isolation, which for the most part, its residents didn't mind. They were happy working in their vineyards, and contact with outsiders beyond necessary business was not needed, or wanted. As one resident wrote: "From their standpoint . . . every new settler, every new business or industry that sought or gained admittance to the colony meant a disturbance of the serene and care-free life to which they

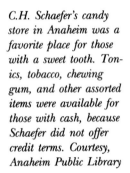

C.H. Schaefer's candy store in Anaheim was a favorite place for those with a sweet tooth. Tonics, tobacco, chewing gum, and other assorted items were available for those with cash, because Schaefer did not offer credit terms. Courtesy, Anaheim Public Library

had accustomed themselves."

Other than the German residents, the only sizeable group was a community of Chinese. As early as 1870 there were about 15 Chinese, but their numbers grew throughout the years. By 1876, one sixth of Anaheim's population was Oriental. In addition to tending truck farms northeast of the colony, they became barbers, tailors, grocers, and laundrymen for the area.

The outside world was starting to

close in. The nearby settlement of Santa Ana, founded in 1869, was growing rapidly. The towns of Orange and Tustin soon followed.

The opening of a Western Union Telegraph office in 1870 established a major communication link to the outside. But the arrival of the Southern Pacific Railroad did the most to break the colony's isolation and to spur growth. The last spike of the railroad's extension from Los Angeles to Anaheim was driven on January 1, 1875. The depot was built a little west of the town on land donated by a group of businessmen. The improved access brought more visitors to the area, many of whom wanted to test the town's reputation as a health resort. It also gave the town's vintners and other businessmen a cheaper and faster way of hauling their goods and led to the town's first regular mail service.

After years of hard work, Anaheim residents were beginning to enjoy prosperity.

Anaheim incorporated for the second time in 1876 by an act of the Los Angeles County Board of Supervisors. Just to make it official, in 1878 the town was once again incorporated by the state legislature.

Among the early acts of the new city's board of trustees was an ordinance making it unlawful to be drunk "to such an extent as to be senseless or to stagger or walk or stand unsteady; or not able to walk or stand at all." When people got drunk in Anaheim's saloons, it was usually not the city's conservative residents, but "outsiders" from surrounding towns.

As often happened in young cities, public officials wore more than one hat. Anaheim's town marshall of the time, Louis Wartenberg, was also tax collector, health officer, jailer, and "public pound keeper." Wartenberg wasn't paid much for his many duties, so on the side he ran a stagecoach line to Silverado, which emerged in 1878 because of a brief mining boom.

Fire protection was a major concern.

Anaheim Fire Company No. 1 had been organized in 1871 after the Planter's Hotel burned down, but some questioned its effectiveness. Two years later the *Gazette* wrote, "About the only effective service we have seen the Fire Department render was the able and determined manner in which they consumed gallons of lager on the occasion of their last parade."

After a disastrous fire in early 1877 destroyed several buildings, city trustees

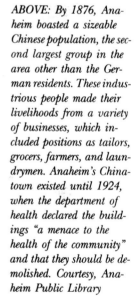

ABOVE: By 1876, Anaheim boasted a sizeable Chinese population, the second largest group in the area other than the German residents. These industrious people made their livelihoods from a variety of businesses, which included positions as tailors, grocers, farmers, and laundrymen. Anaheim's Chinatown existed until 1924, when the department of health declared the buildings "a menace to the health of the community" and that they should be demolished. Courtesy, Anaheim Public Library

LEFT: Ostrich farms were a popular business in early Orange County. Capable of speeds up to 50 miles an hour, these big birds were successful at racing and were favorite circus acts. The two men pictured here are being pulled by the first ostrich ever to be trained in the United States. Courtesy, Anaheim Public Library

Center Street was a thriving business sector back when Anaheim was young. Note the Goodman & Rimpau store, the Bank of Anaheim, Hanna & Keith Real Estate, and of course, the town's Western Union Telegraph Office, which first opened in 1870. Courtesy, Anaheim Public Library

established a new fire department and appointed D.J. Sorenson as fire chief. But even the new department and chief couldn't stop the next major fire, which burned a four-story building co-owned by Sorenson.

Despite such mishaps, Anaheim was a dream coming true in the early 1880s. Years of patient tilling had made the vineyards prosperous indeed. By 1884, 1,250,000 gallons of wine were produced by the colony's 50 wineries. Anaheim was the wine-producing center of Southern California.

Anaheim's vintners had nothing but confidence for their future. Little did they know that in a few short years, their dreams would be destroyed, at least temporarily, by creatures smaller than they could see.

Waging War Over Water

Water was a concern from the beginning for the young wine colony of Anaheim. But despite intermittent droughts, the Santa Ana River proved generally reliable. Household needs were met by backyard wells until 1879, when a municipal water tank and pumping station was built, the

first water distribution system in Orange County.

By the early 1870s, the nearby towns of Santa Ana, Tustin, and Orange had been founded, and the fertile valley on the south side of the river was attracting an increasing number of farmers. The Chapman ditch was dug far north of Anaheim's source to serve the city of Orange in 1870, and was extended six years later by the Semi-Tropic Water Co. to Santa Ana and Tustin.

In 1877 Anaheim colonists noticed that the more northerly ditch was running full while theirs had dwindled to a trickle. The water sank into the sandy riverbed before it reached the irrigation ditches, and vintners had to haul in precious water for their vines in carts. The Anaheim Water Company took the farmers of the new cities to court, arguing that Anaheim's twenty-year-old agreement with Don Bernardo Yorba guaranteed them a ditch full of water.

The costly court battles lasted for years. While the legal war dragged on, another kind of war was also fought along the river. A nasty game of leapfrog ensued, each side trying to draw water from a

LEFT: The arrival of the Southern Pacific Railroad in 1875 helped to establish Anaheim as a prosperous community, and this Orange County railroad station was a busy place for commuters, as well as businessmen shipping their goods to outlying markets. Courtesy, Anaheim Public Library

source higher than the other's. Shotguns and rifles were as much a part of a ditch-digger's equipment as shovels and hoes.

At first a judge agreed with Anaheim and issued an injunction that stopped Semi-Tropic from taking water from the river when it would deprive Anaheim of its rightful "full ditch." Semi-Tropic appealed and, while waiting seventeen months for a ruling, reorganized into the Santa Ana Valley Irrigation Company. But on September 27, 1883, the California Supreme Court reversed the previous ruling, interpreting Anaheim's deed from Yorba as being only for land—not water. The vintners had lost. The warring parties were asked to work out a reasonable solution that would "divide the water on an equitable basis." A compromise was worked out that included the building of a diversion dam at Bedrock Canyon. Connecting ditches were dug, with half the flow going north and west to Anaheim, and the rest going south and west to the other cities.

While Anaheim was battling the towns on the south side of the river, a fight developed on the north side over the Cajon ditch, which was dug by farmers even farther north. Anaheim's lawsuit against the Cajon Irrigation Company finally ended with all interests in the area

consolidating in January 1884 into the Anaheim Union Water Company.

Though the major battles were now over, concern over the lack of water serving the Santa Ana Valley continued. The construction of the Colorado River Water Project in the 1930s and the California State Water Project in the 1950s helped ease the concerns, but the question of where the water will come from for Southern California's continuing growth has yet to be resolved.

ABOVE: Early Anaheim water disputes were settled in January 1884 by consolidating interests into the Anaheim Union Water Company. This company constructed the outlet of the Tuffree Reservoir, pictured here in the late 1800s. Courtesy, Anaheim Public Library

*Orange pickers stop to pose for this 1899 photograph
at the Rimpau Grove located at the corner of what
is now Broadway and Harbour Boulevard. The
Anaheim Public Library stands on this site today.
Courtesy, Anaheim Public Library*

A New Leaf

At first, Anaheim's vintners refused to recognize what was happening to their grapes. The *Anaheim Gazette* reported that 1885 was simply an "off year for Mission grapes." By the next year, however, the newspaper could no longer gloss over the truth. The "vines which appeared vigorous and healthy . . . are beginning to shrivel and dry, and the berries are dropping off," the paper reported.

Before it was finished, the blight that was racing through the colony's vineyards would destroy virtually every vine, forcing all of Anaheim's 50 wineries to become idle. The disease also spread to neighboring cities, infesting vines in Santa Ana, Fullerton, Orange, McPherson, Tustin, and Garden Grove. For most of the Santa Ana Valley, the grape blight was an economic hardship. For wine-dependent Anaheim, it was a catastrophe.

The vintners couldn't see or understand what was turning their once-prosperous vines into diseased waste. The mission grape was at first the only one affected. But soon other varieties succumbed, even wild grapes and raisin grapes. A total of 25,000 acres of vines perished.

On July 24, 1886, a group of growers met in Anaheim's Kroeger's Hall and decided to query University of California professor Eugene W. Hilgard about the disease. Later, Newton B. Pierce, special agent from the U.S. Department of Agriculture, made a thorough study and published a report in 1892, but could not come up with a culprit. It wasn't until 1957 that the source of the problem was discovered. Leafhoppers, creatures too small to be seen by the naked eye were the problem. The insects sucked the juices out of the vines,

causing them to dry and wilt. The insects also carried a virus, which turned out to be more devastating than the leafhoppers themselves. No cure was ever found for what became generally known as "Anaheim disease." It was later renamed "Pierce's disease."

The colonists pulled out every vine, ending the wine-making venture. The dream of John Frohling, Charles Kohler, and George Hansen was over.

Meanwhile, other happenings around the county were about to sweep Anaheim into one of the most frenetic times in the area's history, and distract its residents somewhat from their troubles: the real estate boom of 1887. It started with a vicious rate war between the Southern Pacific and Santa Fe railroads. The latter completed its main line through the Santa Ana Valley that year. The low railroad fares—which made the journey between Kansas City and Los Angeles as cheap as a dollar at one point—lasted about six months. The two rivals finally decided they had lost enough money and called a truce. In the meantime, a real estate boom was ignited that grabbed the county and pulled it on a wild rollercoaster ride. Thousands of tourists from across the nation found their way to Southern California, including many real estate agents. As brass bands played, free luncheons were served, and speculators strove to make a killing, 12 new cities were started in Orange County (then still the southern corner of Los Angeles County). Many saw the boom as a way to end the economic woes caused by the grape blight.

Some Anaheim residents joined the investment frenzy, though most—still feeling the effects of the blight—shied away from

Anaheim High School was the city's first high school. It is pictured here in 1901. Courtesy, Anaheim Public Library

the speculation. Trying to give the city an edge among the many competing towns, a Kansas City public relations man was hired to help promote the city. Anaheim businessmen united with the intent of initiating grand building projects to enhance the city's image. They started with a corporation called the Anaheim Building and Improvement Society. There was relatively little interest, though. The only major project to get off the ground was the huge Hotel del Campo, built by a group of investors for $40,000. With numerous bay windows, fancy balconies, a grand

ballroom, a dining room, and a billiard room, it was a grand structure, but doomed from the start.

Because of a lumber shortage and numerous delays, it was not completed until mid-1888 and wasn't furnished and opened until late 1890. By then, it was too late; the boom was over. The hotel struggled for several years, often with few or no boarders, and in 1896 it became a "Sanitarium and School of Osteopathy." That venture also failed, and it became a cheap lodging house. It was finally torn down in 1905, its lumber used to erect

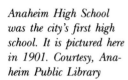

A joint effort between investors in Anaheim and Los Angeles established the Anaheim Street Car Company. Beginning in 1887, the horse-drawn line connected the Southern Pacific depot in the west with the Santa Fe depot on the east side of town. Courtesy, Anaheim Public Library

more than a dozen bungalows.

Another offshoot of the boom was the Anaheim Street Car Company, a joint effort between investors in Anaheim and Los Angeles. Construction began in early 1887 on a horse-drawn line that was to connect the Southern Pacific depot in west Anaheim with the new Santa Fe depot on the east side of town. Though the company began struggling financially soon after it started carrying passengers in March 1887, the venture survived until the fall of 1899.

The boom that started the streetcar line had busted by 1888. The money had dried up, the railroad rate war had ended

in a truce, and the tourists stopped coming. Many of the new towns failed to survive, though Fullerton, Buena Park, and El Toro are reminders of the boom's impact.

Bust or not, leaders in Santa Ana felt it was time for another try at separating from Los Angeles County. Starting with Max von Strobel's crusade in 1870, there had been six efforts over the years, all of them failures. The early attempts were dominated by residents from Anaheim, still the center of the southern corner of Los Angeles County.

But by the late 1870s, Santa Ana had grown into a force to be reckoned with.

Anaheim experienced the need for expanded services and businesses as the result of the 1880s land boom. One such new town business, pictured here with its employees and customers, was Fred Pressel's General Blacksmithing and Horseshoeing establishment. Courtesy, Anaheim Public Library

Santa Ana won the bid to become the county seat of the newly established Orange County in 1889, just one year before this photograph was taken. Although Fourth Street was still unpaved at the time, Santa Ana was a prosperous and growing town whose population surpassed that of Anaheim in the late 1880s. Courtesy, Santa Ana Public Library

While Anaheim leaders still insisted their town should be the county seat of any new county, they renamed it "Santa Ana County" in an 1878 attempt as a concession to its growing challenger. The effort at compromise failed, however, as jealousies over which city should be the county seat helped to scuttle the attempt.

A more elaborate compromise was tried in 1881: The proposed county would be named after Santa Ana, and Anaheim would be the county seat, but only for two years. At that point, any city could vie for the honor, to be decided at the ballot box. The scheme succeeded in creating a united effort—only to die from bad timing. State legislators were occupied that year with the statewide problem of "slickens," or mining debris, and the bill for a Santa Ana County never came to a vote.

In the meantime, Santa Ana was rapidly overtaking Anaheim as the population center of the area. Santa Ana indulged heav-

ily in the boosterism of the day, building a railroad to Newport Bay in 1884. Strobel had proposed a similar railroad from Anaheim to its port at Anaheim Landing 14 years before, but it never came to fruition. The colony largely abandoned the port after the Southern Pacific Railroad came to town in 1875. Some Anaheim leaders began to show concern over such lost opportunities. They formed the Anaheim Immigration Association, which published a 33-page pamphlet in 1885, inviting residents to the city. The pamphlet also explained some of the reasons why they hadn't been arriving in the large numbers other cities were receiving. In the pamphlet, the association confessed that "Anaheim was for so long an isolated section of the county," and that

. . . enough of the old order of things remained to prevent Anaheim from receiving its due proportion of the new element which had been pouring into the county. If this be the true reason

why Anaheim's growth has been more steady than rapid, there is no reason, from this time henceforth, it should not participate largely in whatever progress is made in the County generally. For its people are now as eager to welcome the stranger as they once were to repel him.

But in 1889, it was Santa Ana that led the seventh and final effort to separate from Los Angeles, using the name of "Orange County" and giving the possible secession a new twist. In previous attempts, the dividing line for the new county had been set at the San Gabriel River, but this time it was moved south to Coyote Creek. Anaheim leaders, no doubt preoccupied by their city's problems, didn't notice the boundary change until the legislation was near passage, and then they screamed bloody murder. The new border was only four miles away from Anaheim, ensuring that Santa Ana, not Anaheim,

would be centrally located.

"If the bill had for its purpose the establishment of the county seat at Santa Ana," wrote the *Anaheim Gazette*, "the boundary line could not have been arranged with more effect."

Because of that, when it came time to vote on the new county on June 4, 1889, most Anaheim residents sided with Los Angeles County in opposing it. In the end, however, favorable votes from Santa Ana and other nearby cities carried the day, and the new county was created by a margin of 2,509 to 500. Six weeks later, Santa Ana was voted the county seat.

As disappointed as Anaheim residents may have been, they had greater priority: rebuilding a local economy devastated by the grape blight. Growers replaced their vines with different crops, experimenting to see which would work the best.

Several growers did well, though all

Dating back to its humble beginnings in 1913, the Martenent Hardware Store is a family-owned business that is still a thriving establishment on Center Street in Anaheim. Pictured here in the early 1900s is the store's first location with owner Morris W. Martenent, Sr., visible in the back behind the counter. Courtesy, Anaheim Public Library

Organized on July 15, 1878, the Anaheim Fire Department posed in front of the Anaheim Union High School for this 1916 photograph. Courtesy, Anaheim Public Library

Shown here holding the reins of his homemade Rural Free Delivery mail wagon is Frank Eastman, who established the first of Anaheim's three delivery routes in 1901. These mail routes had previously been covered on foot. Courtesy, Anaheim Public Library

had their problems. One of the most successful crops of the early experiments was the walnut, whose trees took over many of the fields where grape vines once flourished. At one point, Orange County became the walnut shipping center of the world. But soon a series of walnut-destroying pests became widespread enough that farmers turned to other crops.

Chili peppers were also planted in the Anaheim area, starting around 1890. Even though a cooperative attempt at operat-

ing a chili evaporator in Anaheim failed, the tasty peppers were a success over the next few decades. At one point Orange County was growing virtually all of the chili peppers in the state. One of the most popular pepper varieties was a long and slender strain called the Anaheim, in honor of the town of its origin. The industry was destroyed in the 1920s by an invasion of chili weevils.

Other experiments also found some success, including sugar beets, lemons, and apricots. But the crop that would truly help the new county live up to its name—with Anaheim a major contributor—was a late-blooming variety of orange originally called "Hart's Tardiff," but which soon acquired the much more melodious name we know it by: Valencia.

Oranges were practically nonexistent in Orange County during Anaheim's early years. The few that were grown were descendants of trees planted by Franciscan friars in the early eighteenth century, and they were not very tasty. One visitor as late

as 1875 described them as "pithy, sour, thick-skinned and dry . . . an insult to the no-blest of fruit."

By then several locals were trying to change that. The credit for the first orange grove in the county belongs to Dr. William N. Hardin, a physician and Anaheim's justice of the peace, known for his predilection to-ward liquor—he once bragged that he had drunk enough whisky to fill all of the city's irrigation ditches. In 1870, he obtained two barrels of decaying Tahiti oranges and ex-tracted the seeds. He planted them in beds, started the first grove, and soon had a thriv-ing business selling seedlings.

Several varieties were soon being raised in the county, including Mediterra-nean Sweets, St. Michaels, Washington Navels, and Valencias. The latter were carefully cultivated and improved by

Charles C. Chapman of Fullerton, and he is remembered by history as the "father of the Valencia orange industry."

Part of the Valencia's success was due to Chapman's expert marketing, in which he created his own "Old Mission" brand, promoted the Valencia's superiority, and refused to send any to market before they were ready—as some growers did in their rush to reach the Eastern markets.

But it was the Valencia's late-blooming qualities that made it most attractive. There was a strong demand for oranges that ri-pened in the late spring, after the season of the Washington Navel had passed. The juicy Valencia met this criterion as an orange for the thirsty summer buyer far bet-ter than its competitors, keeping its flavor both on and off the tree, and doing so much better in Southern California than

Aside from lemons and oranges, walnuts also proved to be a lucrative venture for Anaheim farmers. Workers at a local walnut grove are pictured here circa 1890, with slatted trays in which the walnuts were laid out to dry in the sun. After an appropriate time, the nuts were polished, graded, and sacked for the marketplace. Courtesy, Anaheim Public Library

ABOVE: The success of Anaheim's orange industry started with Dr. William N. Hardin. Hardin planted and established the first grove in the community, and since then a variety of oranges has developed, including the ever-popular Valencia orange. This Anaheim Board of Trade automobile advertised the Supreme and Mother Colony Brand of oranges, boasting that Anaheim was the "Home of the Finest Sunkist Valencia Oranges." Courtesy, Anaheim Public Library

RIGHT: Charles C. Chapman of Fullerton is often referred to as the "father of the Valencia orange industry." His cultivation and aggressive marketing of this particular variety of orange helped to bring Orange County to the forefront of the booming citrus industry. Courtesy, Anaheim Public Library

elsewhere in the nation.

The timing was right, too. By 1888, the Santa Fe's lines stretched across the length of Orange County, gave the Southern Pacific enough competition to compel it to lower its rates, and made markets in the East and Midwest more accessible. First hundreds, then thousands, of carloads were shipped yearly from the county.

Other growers took Chapman's cue and marketed the fruit aggressively. Some wrapped their oranges in tissue paper printed with guarantees or colorful designs. Colorful labels also graced the shipping crates, and the artistic labels imprinted brand names into the public consciousness and won higher prices. Today the labels are collectors' items.

For all its attributes, the Valencia was not immune to pests. One of the earliest, and most threatening, was the cottony cushion scale, which had seriously infested county groves by 1887. The solution was found in Australia: A natural enemy of the cottony cushion scale called the "Australian Ladybird," or vedalia, was brought to the area. The newcomer succeeded in

bringing the pest under control.

Red and black scale were also serious problems from the beginning. At first, farmers tried caustic washes with whale oil soap or shark oil to try to free the fruit of the menace, but they often hurt the tree more than the scale. Some simply chopped their trees down.

By 1889, when a third of the county's trees had been infected with red scale, farmers turned to fumigating with gas made from cyanide of potassium and sulfuric acid, invented by Anaheim resident D.W. Coquillet. It worked and probably saved the orange industry from a fate similar to that of the grape.

As the new century dawned, the Valencia and other varieties had caused enough prosperity to help people forget the troubled times of the grape blight. According to a 1905 booklet published by the Anaheim Chamber of Commerce:

We have no hesitancy in saying, for the market reports warrant the claim, that no district of even this favored section excels Orange County in the production of this, "the king of all fruits" . . . Oranges from this county have made the record for high prices every year for the past eight years.

Anaheim was a prime beneficiary of the prosperity and justly described itself as the center of the booming Valencia industry. By the 1900 census, steady growth found the city with a population of 1,568. Five years later, it had doubled to 3,250.

Meanwhile, the onetime vintner colony was adding the social and cultural amenities that complete a city. The Anaheim

Many ingenious and inventive marketing schemes were used to promote the importance of the Anaheim citrus industry around the turn of the century. Here, Jessie Darnley holds her trophy after swimming through three tons of oranges at the City Park Pool to capture her title of "Miss Anaheim." Courtesy, Anaheim Public Library

Library Association was established in 1901, and the next year opened the first library in Cornelius Bruce's Candy Kitchen. He was paid $15 a month to dispense books along with his sweets. By 1907 the expanding library had moved into the chamber of commerce building, and later it moved into the first permanent library building, constructed through an Andrew Carnegie grant. Today the restored building, at Anaheim Boulevard and Broadway, is the Anaheim Museum, and it is listed on the national register of historic sites.

The city's first resort was created by a brewer named Friedrich Conrad. He planted cypress, pine, umbrella, and pepper trees next to the big brick building that housed his Anaheim Brewery, and built about a dozen summer homes. Stationary tables and benches were placed near each home, and scattered throughout the park. In the center he built a round pavilion, which included a dance floor. Later would come a bowling alley, a shooting gallery, and a croquet course.

The new resort, which opened in 1876, was called Tivoli Gardens, after the famous Tivoli pleasure gardens of Copenhagen, Denmark. It was later renamed Columbia Gardens. Hundreds of people, many from neighboring towns, gathered in the park on weekends for picnics. They could bring their own food, or buy sandwiches, beer, and soda pop at the brewery. Singing competitions were often held, with groups arriving at the nearby train depot from as far away as San Francisco.

Conrad sold the brewery and the resort in 1904, and the land would change hands several more times before the gardens were sold to the Anaheim Concordia Club. The club, which had started in 1861 as The Liederkranz with 22 members, was made up of German male singers and a *Turnverein,* or a German athletic club.

LEFT: Pictured here in 1911 are Anaheim postal workers. From left to right are Mr. La Gorgue, Robert Johnston, Thomas Hollingworth, postmaster J.W. Duckworth, his daughter Lola Duckworth, and two other unidentified postal carriers. Courtesy, Anaheim Public Library

FACING PAGE: Cornelius Bruce was paid $15 a month to house Anaheim's first library in his Candy Kitchen. By 1907 the library had grown enough to move into the chamber of commerce building, but soon moved again into its first permanent structure at Broadway and Anaheim Boulevard, which now serves as the Anaheim Museum. Courtesy, Anaheim Public Library

In 1922, the club built Concordia Hall, which became a monthly gathering place for games, dancing, and other entertainment. The building became Harmony Hall and later Pepper Tree Faire. Today it is the Whole Earth Marketplace. The Concordia Club continued to grow through the years, and by 1976 it had a membership of 200. The club eventually sold the building because of lack of funds.

Theodore Reiser built an opera house for the city, staging its first performance in 1888, *Ingomar*. Performances were not always high quality, nor the audiences large enough to give Reiser a good return on his investment, but the Anaheim man, who died in 1894, was hailed for his public spirit. The building was often rented for other purposes to help support its shows. It was finally torn down in 1917.

Like much of Orange County, Anaheim still suffered from poor roads as the twentieth century dawned. One settler of the time said that:

the road to Anaheim was just a couple of ruts zigzagging this way and that—not straight like it is now. At some seasons of the year the sunflowers grew so tall and so close to the road that they would touch your hat when driving by. It was half a day's drive to go to Anaheim and back and it required all day for a round trip to Santa Ana.

One solution to the problem was the Pacific Electric Railway, a venture by Henry E. Huntington that started in Long Beach and extended its first line into Orange County to Huntington Beach and Newport Beach in 1905. Within a few years, the electric trains were crisscrossing much of the county, and continued to serve the area for decades to come.

A planned line to Anaheim never materialized. But that would not remain a problem for too many years. Automobiles, not trains, were going to be the county's primary means of transportation.

The first cars arrived in the area soon after the turn of the century. At first, they were regarded as little more than expensive, impractical toys, and the rutted and dusty dirt roads made driving dif-ficult. But as more and more people took to the roads, they began calling for better ones. The Savage Act, passed by the state legislature in 1907, permitted coun-ties to vote bonds for the improvement of the highways.

There was enough opposition at first to delay Orange County's participa-tion for a few years. In 1910, a three-man county highway com-mission was appointed to map and survey the county's roads. Two years later, voters ap-proved a $1.27-million bond issue for im-

provements. By 1917, more than 168 miles had been paved throughout the county, not counting the 43 miles of state highway that con-nected it to its neigh-bors on the north and south. The new roads helped to clear the path for major growth, both economi-cally and in popula-tion, that Anaheim and other cities would experience in the 1920s. It also took the brakes off automobile registra-tions, which climbed in Orange County from 3,761 in 1914 to 9,794 in 1919.

Other modern conveniences helped to bring Anaheim into the twentieth cen-tury. The city's first electric generating sta-

tion began supplying electric lights to businesses in 1895, making Anaheim the first in the county to do so. Street lighting came in 1915, an occasion that prompted a major parade. The mayor and other city officials rode in a car decorated with a miniature street light on each of its corners.

Temperance was a major political issue in the county through the early years of the new century, fueled by the Woman's Christian Temperance Union and religious groups. City after city went dry, though Anaheim voted down a measure that would have closed its saloons. By 1916, Anaheim and Seal Beach were the only "wet" cities left in the county. Three years later, the whole nation went dry through the enactment of Prohibition, which lasted until 1933.

As the years went by Anaheim found itself recovering from its troubled times. A new city hall was built in 1892, and many new businesses were added, including the Anaheim Sugar Factory. The schools grew rapidly. Prior to World War I, Anaheim had four theaters, a hospital, a public library, and a thriving commercial district.

There were also occasional special events. On November 12, 1915, the Liberty Bell arrived for a special stop in Anaheim between exhibitions in San Francisco and San Diego. About 1,500 people came to see the historic bell.

The bright dream of the early 1880s had ended in a nightmare of blight and lost opportunities. But its residents entered a new century full of hope and prosperity once again, this time buoyed by a new crop. There were more hard times to come, but this time Anaheim's leaders were ready for them, primed to grow and determined not to make the mistakes of the past.

But first, there was a war to fight.

Excited residents prepared for Anaheim's Fourth of July celebration along Center Street in 1903. Courtesy, Anaheim Public Library

Before the advent of World War I and the tumultu-
ous years of the 1920s, the 1905 graduating stu-
dents of Anaheim High School dressed in their finest
to pose for this memorable class portrait. Courtesy,
Anaheim Public Library

A Changing World

After the United States formally entered World War I on March 15, 1917, it didn't matter that the ancestry of many Anaheim residents was German. Nor did it matter that outsiders sometimes suspected Anaheim's Germans of being pro-Kaiser, and even of conducting spy activities. When residents were called upon to help the U.S. effort, they always did and always in a big way.

Shortly after America's entry, a "home guard" was formed in Anaheim, and 41 men signed up "for the preservation of peace in this locality and the defense of our homes," the *Anaheim Gazette* wrote. "Some of these boys have gray hair and boast of a number of grand children, but when it comes to a question of fighting in the defense of the Star Spangled Banner they are just as young as they used to be."

On June 5, when citizens were called upon to register for the draft, 350 men reported in Anaheim. "There are no slackers in Anaheim," the *Gazette* wrote afterwards. "They all obeyed the call, came forward willingly and gave such information as was required of them." By the next week, 477 had registered.

Anaheim residents were not happy when the study of German was dropped from the high school curriculum, nor at the occasional shouts of "Hun" in schoolyards. But when residents were asked to pitch in to support the war effort, they did so generously.

Anaheim hosted a benefit dance at Moose Hall for Company L, Santa Ana's National Guard unit. An American Red Cross chapter was founded in April and quickly began cranking out supplies for "our boys," including surgical dressings, sweaters, and socks.

Residents grew "Victory Gardens," and always over-subscribed their Liberty Bonds. Anaheim High School students raised $32,000 towards the war effort selling bonds and other items. As a resident of the time, Charles Kohlenberger, later said:

I don't think there was a German family that didn't support the war by buying American Liberty bonds. Even we kids bought them . . . most every German family here probably bought more Liberty bonds than those of other immigrated races.

The city had no manufacturing industry to speak of, but it did have the Anaheim Aircraft Corporation, started on a shoestring budget by four area businessmen who built training airplanes for the U.S. Aviation Service (later renamed the U.S. Army Air Corps).

Claude and B.H. Sidnam, owners of Anaheim Saxon car agency, provided the facility, while Fullerton banker Fred Krause and his son Howard supplied the financing. Though handicapped from the start by the wartime shortage of airplane parts, and working largely by trial and error, the firm did manage to build two planes—one of which worked—and to train several pilots. After only a few months, the plucky enterprise called it quits after the government banned all civilian flights over the United States.

Almost as quickly as it had begun, the war was over, and Germany surrendered on November 11, 1918. But the biggest surprise was what happened after the

These three Orange County soldiers hammed it up for the camera in this 1918 snapshot during the turbulent World War I years. Courtesy, Costa Mesa Historical Society

war: Anaheim experienced a great population boom.

Thousands of families seeking cheap homes and a mild climate swarmed into Southern California in the early 1920s. Some of them had gotten a glimpse of the area while serving at local military bases. Orange County, and Anaheim, received many of the new arrivals. The board of supervisors did nothing to discourage them, publishing a booklet that extended a "hearty welcome" to the "Biggest Little County in the State."

Starting in 1920, and continuing unabated for the next four years, the influx nearly doubled Anaheim's population from the 5,526 counted in the 1920 census. Large sections of land adjacent to the city were annexed and quickly subdivided.

The growth was so rapid that city officials had trouble keeping up. Seeing the need for a larger city hall, voters passed a $75,000 bond in 1921 to build a new one. Work on the two-story building, the city's third city hall, began on the same site as its predecessor, built in 1892. But the stream of new residents was so

rapid it quickly became clear an even larger building was needed. A second bond, for $40,000, was passed. The structure was designed in a classical Greek style, based on a building on Athen's Acropolis. After it was finally completed in June 1923, residents were invited to an evening open house to "inspect" it. About 2,000 people, or about a third of the city's population at the time, took the city up on the offer and swarmed into the new building.

The area's Valencia orange industry was also booming. To help showcase both it and the city to tourists and home-seekers, the Anaheim Chamber of Commerce created the California Valencia Orange Show, the first of its kind in the county. The first show opened on May 17, 1921, as President Warren G. Harding's voice crackled over 3,900 miles of wire from Washington, D.C., to the huge tent housing the 11-day affair.

The orange show became an annual affair, held on the present site of La Palma Park. Prizes were given not only for the best exhibits, but also to the packing house with the speediest box packer, with competitors representing the county's orange packing houses. Attendance grew year after year.

The growth of the early 1920s produced other improvements. The city's business section prospered. Development of the first city park began on the site of an orange grove in 1921. The 20-acre Anaheim City Park was unlike any other in the county, furnished with such amenities as a lily pond, swimming pool, lighted baseball diamond, tennis courts, croquet courts, and horseshoe rings.

The city's first parks director, who worked to nurse the Anaheim City Park to life and maintain it for years, was Rudy Boysen. But Boysen is more famous for his horticultural endeavors. In 1925, he crossed a blackberry and a loganberry and

The Kohlenbergers were a prominent family during Anaheim's World War I years. Courtesy, Anaheim Public Library

came up with a new fruit. Later he was visited by a man named Walter Knott, who dubbed the new fruit a "boysenberry" and marketed it vigorously as part of his berry farm in nearby Buena Park.

The city's annual Halloween Parade began in 1924, partly as a way to show

Still a familiar name today, the Sparkletts water company displayed its goods at the 1921 California Valencia Orange Show in Anaheim. Courtesy, Anaheim Public Library

civic pride, but mostly to redirect the energies of local youngsters. Local merchants had grown weary of Halloween pranks, which included the scrawling of graffiti on storefront windows, the overturning of outhouses, and the perching of buggies on top of barn roofs. Organized by the chamber of commerce, the first parade consisted of floats, cars, bands, and drums corps, all stretching for about two miles, according to the *Gazette*. People showed up in costume, and baseball stars Babe Ruth and Walter Johnson, in town for an exhibition, shared the honors as grand marshals.

The parade has grown over the years and has become part of an annual festival that includes a carnival, pancake breakfast, tennis tournament, costume ball, and international food fair and attracts tens of thousands from all over the county.

The basic core of German families that could trace their origins to the city's wine-making days remained relatively intact, but the tremendous influx of new residents brought diversity to Anaheim. And diversity was not all good. Lurking beneath the boomtimes brought by some of

the newcomers were the seeds of the worst political turmoil in the city's history. It could be spelled with three letters: KKK.

The Ku Klux Klan that dominated Anaheim's political scene in the mid-1920s was actually a revival of the movement that had spread terror after the Civil War. Starting in the Deep South in about 1915, the new version of the Klan spread to several parts of the nation. It failed to catch on in western states, except for Southern California.

By 1922, Los Angeles had three klaverns and even a Ku Klux Klan Marching Band, which marched in local parades. From Los Angeles, the Klan spread to several cities in the Southland, including Huntington Beach, Santa Monica, Redondo Beach, Brea, Fullerton, Santa Ana, and Huntington Beach. Anaheim was the last to experience a surge in Klan activity, but also the most affected by it.

The Klan's influence in Anaheim apparently began in 1922 when the Reverend Leon Myers arrived and became pastor of the Anaheim Christian Church. Within a year he started the Men's Bible Club, which became a

ABOVE: Patriotic holidays such as the Fourth of July, Memorial Day, and Labor Day were cause for festive community celebrations enjoyed by all residents, young and old alike. This local Anaheim band donned elaborate uniforms and stood ready for its musical march through town in the 1920s. Courtesy, Anaheim Public Library

FACING PAGE, TOP: Established by the Anaheim Chamber of Commerce to promote the area's Valencia orange industry, the first California Valencia Orange Show opened on May 17, 1921. Courtesy, Anaheim Public Library

FACING PAGE, BOTTOM: The Blue Goose exhibit won the sweepstakes prize at the first California Valencia Orange Show in Anaheim in the spring of 1921. Courtesy, Anaheim Public Library

A revival of the violent and racist movement that had spread terror in the South after the Civil War, the Ku Klux Klan influence on Anaheim's political scene in the 1920s aimed toward psychological conversion rather than relying on physical violence. These unmasked Ku Klux Klan members were photographed while driving through town, petitioning all interested parties to attend their lecture and meeting later that evening. Courtesy, Anaheim Public Library

front for the Klan in Anaheim. Early in 1924, it made its first political foray by accusing the city recorder of inefficiency and of drinking—the latter considered a serious accusation in this age of Prohibition. Though the county grand jury refused to take any action against the official, he resigned anyway, claiming he had been threatened with bodily harm.

The Klan was still a relatively unknown organization in town, with little real influence. Seeking to expand its power, Myers and local Klan leaders secretly backed a slate of four candidates to fill four seats on the city's board of trustees (today's city council), two of them recently vacated by resignations. The four were endorsed by the *Plain Dealer*, Anaheim's leading newspaper and now a clandestine mouthpiece for the Klan. Several

issues dominated the campaign that followed, including the need for stronger law enforcement. That the Klan was involved was hardly mentioned. All four Klan-backed candidates were swept into office in the election on March 3, 1924.

If Anaheim voters did not realize then they were voting for the Klan, they soon found out what it was like having the Ku Klux Klan running the city. The letters "KIGY"—"Klansman I Greet You"—were painted on major streets near the city's borders. Motorists caught speeding by the Klan-controlled police department could escape tickets by proving they were Klan members. Merchants who were KKK members gave discounts to fellow members.

There were few minorities, so Klan leaders directed most of their attacks against Catholics. A burning cross was found in front of St. Boniface Roman Catholic Church. On another occasion its entry doors and keyholes were so thoroughly tarred, they wouldn't open.

The Anaheim Klan of the 1920s was, to be fair, not as monstrous as the Klan of Reconstruction. Its violence was more psychological than physical. The new version won members through a deceptive message of Americanism, patriotism, and fear. Many saw what they wanted to see in the Klan, and it pandered to the fears of those who believed that Catholics, alcohol, and waves of foreign immigrants posed a threat to the American way of life. Many who joined did not see the Klan for its bigoted goals until later.

After the town flagpole mysteriously disappeared from its traditional spot at Anaheim's central intersection, many older residents petitioned to have it returned, but were refused. The flagpole reappeared inside Anaheim City Park. On July 29, 1924, about 800 figures in robes marched down city streets and converged on the park for the largest and most open Klan demonstration in Southern California history. Watched by a crowd estimated at 20,000 people— most of them curious onlookers—the Klansmen held ceremonies and gave speeches. Two airplanes flew overhead, one flashing "KKK" and the other a huge glowing cross, and a cross was burned on the ground.

Spurred by this and other Klan activities, Anaheim's old guard of German families began a drive to rid the city of the Klan. After defeating all the KKK candidates for county, state, and federal offices in the August election, they banded into the USA Club—standing for "Unison, Service, Americanism"—and collected enough signatures to force a recall election of all four Klan trustees. The Klan retaliated by petitioning a recall against the one remaining non-Klan trustee. An

election for all five seats was set for February 3, 1925.

The campaign was a bitter one. The *Plain Dealer* continued to back the four Klan-supported candidates. Helping to gird the forces against the Klan were the *Anaheim Bulletin* and the *Gazette,* now a weekly. Neither side pulled any punches. When the *Plain Dealer*'s publisher encountered family problems, which included a divorce, the *Bulletin* ran story after story offering the details. After *Bulletin* publisher Ernest Louden was physically struck by a Klan supporter, the *Plain Dealer* chortled that he "ran like a deer." The *Bulletin* retorted that the incident signalled the beginning of Klan terrorism.

In any case, the tide had turned

This notice advertising a lecture by the Reverend Leon Myers was the Ku Klux Klan's subtle attempt to discredit perceived opposition. Shortly after arriving in Anaheim in 1922, the Reverend Myers became the pastor of the Anaheim Christian Church. He later established the Men's Bible Club, which actually became a front for the Klan's activity in the city. Courtesy, Anaheim Public Library

against the Klan. A membership list slipped into the hands of USA Club leaders, who distributed copies. Only 300 names were on the list—far fewer than the 1,000 claimed by the Klan—and they included the names of the four city trustees.

Aided by a remarkable 90-percent-voter turnout, anti-Klan forces won a clear victory in the recall, unseating all four KKK-backed trustees while preventing the recall of the lone non-Klan trustee.

The victory was complete. The *Plain Dealer* was besieged by a libel lawsuit filed by Reverend James A. Geissinger, a Methodist pastor and long a target of the Klan's accusations. A few months after the recall, the paper published a front-page apology

to Geissinger, then promptly folded.

The Klan never again played a major role in Anaheim. Still, the city needed years to recover. Lengthy boycotts by both sides had crippled the city's economic climate. As Klan businessmen went elsewhere, their shops stayed empty for months, even years. Some people left the city, and many prospective residents settled elsewhere. The wounds did not heal easily.

In an effort to foster harmony, the city formed a baseball commission that sponsored play between Anaheim's team and others from Santa Ana, Whittier, Long Beach, and Fullerton, with games played in Anaheim City Park. The league drew a great deal of attention, and some games

attracted between 4,000 to 5,000 spectators. "I think it did more to bring order out of chaos than anything else we could have done," Charles Pearson, a city planning commissioner at the time and later mayor, remembered years later.

Another bright spot, as Anaheim finished the 1920s, was the citrus industry, which continued to boom in and around the city. In 1923, Orange County boasted 37,528 acres of Valencias, which produced 4.3 million boxes of oranges worth $10.9 million. By 1930, the totals had grown to 44,449 acres, 5 million boxes of oranges, and a value of $35.7 million.

Still, prosperity never came too easily for orange growers, who fought a constant battle against pests. The dreaded scale insect had been brought under control by fumigation, but was soon followed by the mealybug, which invaded the Anaheim area and infected tens of thousands of trees. This time, the solution was found in nature. A predator of the mealybug, the Australian ladybug, was shipped to Anaheim, raised in an "insectory" on Vermont Street, and released in afflicted areas, bringing the mealybug under control.

The area's Mediterranean climate was a boon to growers, but did not always cooperate. The mercury occasionally fell too low for oranges. Below 28 degrees, oranges could suddenly turn tasteless and dry. In the big frost of 1913, when the mer-

The many thriving orange groves in early twentieth-century Anaheim carried on the successful citrus industry that was first established in the late 1800s. Courtesy, Anaheim Public Library

cury dipped to 22 degrees three nights in a row, growers burned bean straw in the groves in a futile effort to keep the oranges from freezing. Later, they turned to smudge pots. Advertised as "smokeless orchard heaters," the diesel-burning smudge pots were anything but smokeless. Housewives saw the black fumes darken their drapes and furnishings, but realized the smudge pots were necessary. On cold nights, thousands of smudge pots were set burning, spaced throughout the groves for maximum effect. Smudging was very expensive, and annoying, but farmers had little choice. Their crops, and the livelihood of the county, were at stake.

According to Samuel Armor in his 1921 history of the county, the "Valencia Late"

. . . as it has been developed here, is the best orange grown in the world. For more than twenty years it has made the record for prices

received for California oranges. It has many excellent qualities which make it a most desirable and profitable orange for grower, handler and consumer . . . It has been the most popular orange with growers for many years, and especially in Orange County, which seems to be able to produce this splendid variety more perfectly than any other section of the state.

Despite the area's success with Valencias, Anaheim business leaders saw early that the city could not rely on the orange forever. On February 28, 1924, the Community Industrial Land Company was incorporated by leaders of the Anaheim Chamber of Commerce, with the aim of diversifying the city's economic base.

The group raised $40,000 in private money, bought up the land left vacant by the now closed Anaheim Sugar Factory, and created the North Anaheim Industrial Tract. The land, located on 40 acres north

Participants in the Old Timers Picnic pose for their portrait on June 11, 1927, at Anaheim City Park. Among these descendents of California's first settlers is Francesca Mosserman in the wheelchair, the only surviving pioneer who settled in Anaheim in 1857. Mosserman celebrated her 92nd birthday just before the picnic. Courtesy, Anaheim Public Library

of La Palma Avenue, was sold for reduced prices to entice industry. It managed to attract a few new firms. The first was the United States Alcohol plant. Others included a juice and concentrate factory and a paint base manufacturer.

The tract was later expanded to 416 acres, and today forms the nucleus of Anaheim's North Central Heavy Industrial district, though none of the original firms remain. At the time, it was the only industrial area in Southern California outside of

the task of helping to guide future growth.

Despite the slowdown that followed the temporary rule of the Ku Klux Klan, city leaders were confident that such problems were behind them as the 1920s drew to a close. Anaheim was the center of the area's vibrant Valencia orange industry, and had the beginnings of an industrial zone. There were 19 miles of paved streets—seven of them decorated with ornamental street lights—17 churches, 10 schools, 2,635 telephones, and a popula-

Former teammates greet legendary pitcher Walter Johnson in Anaheim during his exhibition tour in 1926. Courtesy, Anaheim Public Library

Los Angeles. Still, the effort to attract industry was only a minor success, and it was not until the 1950s that another post-war boom transformed Anaheim into a major industrial center. The land company continued until it dissolved in 1966.

Another act of foresight taken by city trustees, in early 1927, was the creation of the first municipal planning commission in Orange County. Five members were appointed to the new planning body by the trustees on February 10, 1927, entrusted with

tion that totaled 10,995 in the 1930 census. The orange show was attracting 150,000 visitors annually.

City leaders were eager to put the unpleasant experience with the Klan behind them. And, as the 1930s dawned, that finally seemed possible. But happenings in a place back East that few residents thought much about—Wall Street—soon told Anaheim residents that their dreams were not going to come true—not yet, anyway.

Many families came to Southern California to escape the harsh Dust Bowl of the Midwest in the 1930s. This Missouri family was photographed in 1936 as they made their way through the state looking for work and a place to call home. Courtesy, Library of Congress

The Great Slowdown

When the stock market crashed on October 28, 1929, most Anaheim residents didn't show much concern. Nor did most people in Orange County. The region was still mostly agricultural, and locals were not really the type to speculate in the stock market.

As late as December 1930, an editorial in the *Anaheim Gazette* assured its readers that "Things Are Looking Up," despite the deepening economic crisis. While admitting that "It has been a tough year; there is no denying that," it blamed the nation's problems on "timidity," and affirmed that the problems would end just as soon as people began opening their wallets and spending again.

Orange County was not as hard-hit by the Great Depression as other parts of the nation, but the economic problems were nonetheless worse than any it had seen before. Unemployment soared as high as 15 percent and persisted as a serious problem throughout the 1930s.

In the early years, Anaheim and other cities tried to find their own solutions to the joblessness and the itinerants who roamed the streets, even knocking on doors as they sought food and shelter. The city's first response, in the winter of 1930-31, was to house itinerants in the city jail at night. It contracted with a nearby cafe to provide supper and breakfast to those who agreed to "move on" afterward. As many as 47 in one night used the jail for temporary lodgings.

The next winter, the city turned over such relief work to the Salvation Army. Vagrants could earn shelter for the night and two meals by sweating over a woodpile for two hours. Those refusing were shown the city border.

The city hired about 200 jobless men to make improvements in the water system. That was soon expanded into the "Anaheim Plan," a novel scheme originated by local merchants in which the unemployed were paid for public projects with certificates redeemable at participating stores. The city provided the work, which included reinforcing the Santa Ana River dikes, shoring up of an old wash north of the city, and digging underground canals to replace surface irrigation ditches. In practice, the Anaheim Plan proved a bit cumbersome and didn't last, but civic leaders still lauded it as an exemplary local attempt to deal with the bleak employment picture.

In the summer of 1932, growers in the area provided the needy with a part of their perishable surplus of fruits and vegetables in return for help in harvesting the more marketable portion.

The city had already started to whittle down its tax rate in the late 1920s, and continued through most of the 1930s as city officials tried to ease the tax burdens of homeowners who otherwise might have lost their homes. At the time, city officials could decrease no more than 10 cents a year off the rate. The tax rate stood at $1.45 for $100 of valuation in 1927, but by 1936 it was only 70 cents, the lowest rate in the state. In turn, the city budget steadily shrank. Among the cost-cutting measures was a reduction of city salaries by 10 percent for its 42 employees at the end of 1931, and the elimination of the city manager position the next year.

The position of city manager, which

RIGHT: *The flow of Dust Bowl refugees to Southern California caused a noticeable strain on social services by the late 1930s. Courtesy, Library of Congress*

FACING PAGE: *Migrant families desperate for work, labored in the fields of Southern California for wages as low as 10 cents during the Depression. Courtesy, Bancroft Library*

had been created in 1918, first became an issue in the 1930 municipal campaign. A slate of three candidates emerged pushing for abolition of the post, which they called expensive, inefficient, and unresponsive to the people since it was not an elected position. In answer, the "Citizens Harmony Ticket" was created, asking voters to retain the city manager form of government, while generally calling for more cooperation in the city. On April 14, 75 percent of the city's voters went to the polls, siding with the Harmony ticket by a large margin.

Two years later, the city manager position was no longer an issue, but after the 1932 election, municipal finances were. The city clerk had abruptly resigned, and instead of picking a successor the council unexpectedly voted to abolish the city manager's job. Longtime city manager John W. Price took over the job of city clerk and street superintendent, a move that saved the city about $500 monthly. The city went without any kind of overall administrator until 1950 and

without a city manager until 1956.

But cost-cutting and local programs for the jobless were not nearly enough to shake the economic woe that had descended on the area. The depth of dissatisfaction was shown in the sudden willingness of Anaheim voters, who traditionally scorned any kind of state or federal help, to forsake deep-seated party allegiances in their cry for help. In the 1928 presidential race, Republican Herbert Hoover carried every precinct in Anaheim, as Republican candidates normally did. But decades of Republican loyalty ended in 1932, as all but five of Anaheim's twenty-four precincts went to Democrat Franklin D. Roosevelt and his promise to rejuvenate the nation's economy.

The alphabet soup of agencies created by Roosevelt's New Deal provided jobs for tens of thousands in Orange County, including several projects in Anaheim. A Works Progress Administration (WPA) project built a new 17-acre park on the site of the old orange show in 1936. The chamber of commerce offered a $25 cash

prize for the best name for the new park. Seven people turned in the winning name of La Palma, and split the prize.

After a delay caused by destruction from a 1938 flood, the new park was dedicated in August 1939. Its baseball field was considered one of the best in the nation, good enough to lure Connie Mack and his Philadelphia Athletics to use it

for spring training from 1940 through 1942. The practices only halted with the beginning of World War II and the imposition of wartime restrictions on team travel. Later it was used as a training ground for the St. Louis Browns in 1946 and the minor-league Hollywood Stars practiced there in the 1950s. In combination with Anaheim City Park, La Palma

In cooperation with the Public Works of Art Administration, artist Arthur Forbes Ames painted this 15-foot mural portraying his perception of everyday life in Anaheim. The mural was on exhibit at the Anaheim Public Library in 1934. Ames also painted two other murals for the Newport Harbor High School. Courtesy, Anaheim Public Library

Park and others that followed gave the city recreational areas that were the envy of Orange County.

The Public Works of Art Administration produced two works of art for Anaheim. One was a statue of Madame Helena Modjeska, created by Eugen Maier-Krieg and unveiled at Anaheim City Park on September 15, 1935. Another was a 15-foot mural painted by Arthur Ames through Civil Works Administration funds. Ames also did two murals for Newport Harbor High School.

Another project extended Anaheim's electrical distribution system. But perhaps the most badly needed federal project was the WPA-supported extension of Metropolitan Water District lines. The city had long depended on wells for its domestic supply, and the water level had dropped 87 feet between 1916 and the early 1930s, down to 137 feet.

Such programs helped to lessen much of the desperation of the times, but the 1930s were a constant struggle for most people. The miseries were added to by a pair of natural disasters that left Anaheim and the rest of Orange County hard hit. The first was the 1933 earthquake, which shook the area for 15 furious seconds on March 10. Nearly all of the 120 deaths occurred in the more populous Long Beach area, but Orange County counted four dead and millions of dollars in property damage. Chimneys collapsed, streets cracked, and buildings were damaged. In Anaheim, many streets were covered with debris, particularly in the business section. Schools were badly damaged, and students had to attend classes in temporary army barracks for a long time. The second catastrophe was the flood of 1938. A series of storms swelled the Santa Ana River, which

Dedicated in August 1939, the 17-acre La Palma Park featured one of the best baseball fields in the country. Used as a training ground over the years for the Philadelphia Athletics, the St. Louis Browns, and the Hollywood Stars, La Palma Park is shown here in a 1948 aerial view. Courtesy, Anaheim Public Library

The ground shook for what seemed to be an eternity for 15 seconds on March 10, 1933, bringing death and destruction to Orange County. Many structures were badly damaged in Anaheim and surrounding areas, including this establishment in Buena Park. Courtesy, Anaheim Public Library

The 1933 earthquake wreaked havoc on Baker's Bakery and Ketner's Confectionery in Anaheim, littering the streets with ruin and debris. Courtesy, Anaheim Public Library

shortly after midnight on March 3 breached its banks and roared through much of the county. The flood carried away many homes, cars, and bridges with its force. Reaching a depth of four to five feet in parts of Anaheim, the water entered homes and forced some residents to seek refuge on top of pianos, tables, and kitchen ranges, and even on roofs. A total of 19 lives were lost, and thousands of acres of agricultural land were badly damaged.

After the flood, the city arranged to haul away any mud that residents and business owners could move out to the curb. As with the earthquake, city service clubs, physicians, and other residents assisted with the cleanup and injuries. Because classrooms had been flooded, students again had to be moved to temporary quarters.

The flood reminded local officials of the hazards of living on a flood plain, and the Prado Dam was built in Riverside County to help lessen the effects of future deluges. It was completed in 1941.

Even the area's indefatigable orange industry was not totally immune from economic travails. By 1930, attendance at the city's annual Valencia orange show had begun to falter. The last hurrah came the next year, when neighboring communities joined Anaheim in staging the Orange County Valencia Orange Show and Fair.

As growers felt the pressures of falling prices, they dumped tons of the smaller, less marketable oranges into the Santa Ana River bed, spraying them with oil to prevent would-be peddlers from trying to sell them.

Despite the problems, which also included occasional labor unrest, the area's groves remained among the most productive in the world, and expanded through much of the decade. By 1938, the Valencia's peak, 67,536 acres were planted. The groves produced more than 9.3 million boxes, worth $16.9 million.

The real trouble on the horizon had nothing to do with the Depression. It was a new disease called "quick decline," named for the speed with which it killed orange trees. Another name, just as descriptive, was *tristeza,* Portuguese for grief, gloom, or sorrow.

First detected in Southern California in 1939, the disease was raging through Orange County's orange groves within just a few years. The malady was finally traced

in 1946 to a virus carried by the melon aphid, but no cure was ever found. As late as the early 1960s, quick decline killed 243,920 orange trees in the county in just a six-month period.

Anaheim voters had again voted for Roosevelt in 1936. The only Republican to win a partisan office in Orange County was Anaheim's Thomas Kuchel, who won a state assembly seat. Kuchel went on to have a distinguished career, serving as a U.S. senator and senate minority leader. He was also elected state controller, and served as state Republican party chairman three times.

The effects of the Depression persisted into the early 1940s, but politics in Anaheim and the rest of Orange County were beginning to return to normal again. Local voters felt that New Deal politics had taken too radical a turn. Both the city and

Hundreds of spectators from throughout Orange County turned out to greet President Franklin D. Roosevelt in nearby Laguna Beach in 1938— a jubilant moment that helped to inspire hope for the future during the difficult Depression era. Courtesy, Historical Collection, First American Title Insurance Company

the county voted against Roosevelt in 1940.

The bombing of Pearl Harbor on December 7, 1941, soon made everyone forget about both politics and their economic troubles.

Anaheim, which seven months earlier had established the first of several defense councils formed in the county, went to work enrolling and instructing air raid wardens, auxiliary police and firemen, and other civil defense workers. During blackouts, all blinds had to be closed, and lights turned off. Cars were equipped with dim "blackout lights."

In case of emergency, a system was developed for sending school children home along "safe" routes, escorted by auxiliary police traffic wardens.

Anaheim still had a large German population, but both city officials and citizens made it clear that the city's residents were fully behind the war effort. City Attorney Leo J. Friis insisted that the council intended "to handle every situation arising from the war in a sensible manner and to do all in its power to maintain a rational

attitude towards all persons of foreign descent." Similarly, a letter published in the *Santa Ana Register* from an Anaheim resident stressed, "Many of us have Japanese and German neighbors. As long as they remain loyal to our country, let us be loyal to them."

A curfew and travel restrictions were imposed on all German and Italian aliens and all Japanese on March 27, 1942. Shortly afterward, Exclusionary Orders stated that all Japanese in the county had to be registered at sites in Anaheim, Huntington Beach, and San Onofre. They were then shipped to the Poston Relocation Center in Arizona. Though they were later allowed to return, many no longer had any home to return to.

The county's National Guard units, including Company K of Anaheim, were inducted into federal service nine months before the attack on Pearl Harbor. Later, as part of the 40th Division, Company K distinguished itself in the Philippines at the Battle of the Seven Hills on Luzon island and again at Panay island.

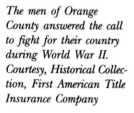

The men of Orange County answered the call to fight for their country during World War II. Courtesy, Historical Collection, First American Title Insurance Company

Rationing was a fact of life in wartime Anaheim, with rationed items including sugar, coffee, shoes, gasoline, and many foods. Many residents grew their own food in backyard "Victory Gardens."

Many people joined the Army or worked for high wages in the factories that were retooling for the nation's defense. The result was an acute shortage of farm labor. Without enough men to harvest the orange crop, representatives of 41 of the county's 45 orange packing houses met at the Anaheim Elks Clubhouse and heard a plan to import seasonal workers from Mexico. Under the resulting bracero program, 1,650 Mexicans arrived in 1943. The program was expanded the next year, including 1,600 Jamaicans. In late 1945, 563 German prisoners of war were assigned to the orchards and other duties.

The manpower shortage was so severe that Anaheim Union High School students occasionally were given half-day schedules so they could help out at harvest time, or work in local stores at Christmastime.

With help from imported workers,

the Valencia industry continued to do well through the war. But as the war ended, and the nation began to adjust once again to peacetime, it was quickly becoming clear that the future of Anaheim did not lay in Valencia oranges. The massive influx of new residents and new industries was about to begin the process that would change the city forever, followed closely by a mouse that would put Anaheim on the map.

Local Orange County servicemen and their companions gather to celebrate the Christmas holidays in the early 1940s. Courtesy, Costa Mesa Historical Society

Cadets at the Santa Ana Army Air Base undergo testing in the decompression chamber in 1943. Courtesy, Historical Collection, First American Title Insurance Company

Civic leaders in Anaheim were able to foresee the post-war boom of the 1940s and 1950s and helped to create an atmosphere that was conducive to industrial growth and development. Earne Moeller was hired by the Anaheim Chamber of Commerce in 1945 to lead the promotional efforts. He is pictured here on the right shaking hands with Hal Gregg at an unidentified event at the town's city hall. Courtesy, Anaheim Public Library

Dreams Come True

Before the 1950s, the only time most people across the nation ever heard of Anaheim was during Jack Benny's popular radio show, where the comedian made it a station on his imaginary "Anaheim, Azusa & Cucamonga Railroad." The city didn't mind the connection at all—it even made Benny an honorary mayor.

Anaheim was still a relatively small, close-knit community with its biggest industry still in its orange groves. But all that would change with incredible speed in a post-World War II boom that not only doubled the city's population several times over, but made it a world-class tourist attraction.

The remarkable boom was unlike anything Anaheim or the rest of Southern California had ever seen. It was a never-ending flood, starting slowly in the late 1940s and becoming a mad rush in the 1950s. Anaheim, which entered the 1950s with a population of 14,556, grew to an astounding 104,184 only a decade later, according to census figures. Anaheim became the fastest-growing city in the nation, leading a county that was also the fastest-growing in the United States.

The roots of Anaheim's transformation from a quiet agricultural community into a fast-growing center of industry and entertainment lay in the war itself, and what was happening around the city. No less than half a dozen military bases sprang up in Orange County during the war, and hundreds of thousands of servicemen spent time there, either in training or to be processed after the war. The close look they got of the area's mild climate, shimmering beaches, and many acres of orange trees was enough to

convince many of them to come back— which they did by the droves.

Other factors fueled the boom, including cheap land, low housing costs, and low interest rates that averaged four percent for conventional loans, and went down as low as two percent for veterans who joined the service in California. Improved transportation also helped, as the growing popularity of the automobile and the building of the Santa Ana Freeway—right through Anaheim—in the 1950s made it easy for newcomers to get there.

Civic leaders saw the boom coming early, and aggressively made sure Anaheim was the county's prime beneficiary. The Anaheim Chamber of Commerce, looking for someone to lead the promotion of the city as a hospitable place for industry, hired Earne Moeller as its manager in 1945. The city also acted, hiring a consultant near the end of the war to develop a general plan. Anaheim, which had abolished the city manager post in 1932, hired Keith Murdock to be city administrator in 1950 to help cope with the enormous changes that had only started. Murdock, elevated to the title of city manager six years later, would head the city's operations until 1976.

Filling out the triumvirate of Anaheim leaders who helped to direct the dizzying growth of the 1950s was Charles Pearson, who had been mayor of the city since 1936 and continued in that role until he resigned in 1959. Nebraska-born, a World War I veteran, and owner of Anaheim Truck and Transfer, the largest trucking firm in the county, Pearson's contacts and skills made him the most influential leader in the city's history.

Pearson, Moeller, and Murdock were

RIGHT: Charles Pearson's tenure as mayor of Anaheim began in 1936 and lasted 24 years until he resigned in 1959. Owner of Anaheim Truck and Transfer, the largest trucking company in Orange County, Pearson was one of the most influential leaders in Anaheim's history. Courtesy, Anaheim Public Library

Hired as city administrator by the Anaheim Chamber of Commerce in 1950, Keith Murdock is joined by other city officials during a meeting at the Emergency Operations Center in the 1950s. Courtesy, Anaheim Public Library

determined to make Anaheim an industrial giant. At first, they had little competition. As Murdock remembered in a magazine interview years later:

Anaheim really made up its mind early to go after industrial and business growth. When I got there the rest of Orange County's cities thought they would go broke if they took a chance on industry. They wanted to be bedroom cities. But it's industry that pays the city's bills through taxes, and it's industry that provides jobs for city residents.

The city's strategy to let industry know it was welcome in Anaheim started with the placement of advertisements in the *Wall Street Journal* and other major publications around the nation. When owners of prospective industries showed interest, they were guided through a series of high-level talks with city officials, ending with the mayor,

in which the advantages of locating in Anaheim were stressed. The Community Industrial Land Company, created by the chamber of commerce in 1924 to entice industry with cheap land, played a new, revived role. The city's strategy also stressed sensible planning, making sure that water lines, sewers, and utilities were ready before the newcomers moved in.

Anaheim also had to sell the idea of industry to its residents, some of whom feared it would bring a "smokestack" image to the town. After Kwikset Locks, the first major industry to locate in the city, opened its doors with 800 employees in 1948, Moeller arranged public tours of the shiny new plant. Later efforts included "Industrial Education Days," in which local teachers and clergymen became guests at different industries. The protests from citrus growers, who saw their industry being pushed out of the city, were muted first by education efforts and later by the huge windfalls they could make by selling their land. Land prices escalated from about $2,750 an acre in 1947, to $6,000 by 1954, to up to $20,000 by 1960.

The city made special efforts to entice the defense industry, which had settled in the eastern end of Los Angeles County during World War II. Several now began expanding into Orange County, where land was cheaper and the labor supply was growing rapidly. The first of the major ones to arrive was Northrop Nortronics (now Northrop Corp.'s Electro-Mechanical division), which opened its Anaheim plant with 2,000 employees in 1951. In 1959, Rockwell International (then North American Aviation) located

its Autonetics Electronics Systems plant in the city.

A wide variety of other companies also came to Anaheim, representing a wide range of industries, including Robertshaw-Fulton Controls Company, the Essex Wire Company, and the General Electric Company.

Making it even easier for business and industry to make the move, Murdock created a "super stamp" system by which developers could begin construction immediately, without first going through the long delays of submitting plans and having

In 1947, Anaheim had 27 independent industries, employing 1,400 workers. By 1968, there were 460 industries, with a total of 48,500 workers.

The post-war world also benefited the city's sizeable Mexican-American population, estimated at a quarter of the city's population. The vast majority of them had worked in the fields or in citrus packing houses in the area, but many earned jobs in the area's defense-related factories during World War II, and afterwards worked in the many industries that opened new plants in and around the city.

Kwikset Locks was the first major industry to locate in Anaheim when it opened its doors in 1948 with more than 800 employees. Courtesy, Anaheim Public Library

them checked. If routine inspections later on turned up problems, the developer was obligated to fix it. As the frenetic building pace continued, city inspectors often worked nights and weekends, with developers picking up the tab for overtime pay.

Anaheim became the county's industrial leader and possessed the fastest-growing industrial base in the nation. By 1970, Anaheim had set aside some 4,300 acres for industrial use, or 20 percent of the city's land. It was more than any of the county's other cities, which by then were following Anaheim's lead in setting aside large tracts for industry.

Anaheim grew in other ways, too. On October 14, 1955, the Broadway opened a three-story, 200,000-square-foot department store at Euclid near the Santa Ana Freeway. It marked the beginning of the first regional shopping center in Orange County. The shopping center—later called Anaheim Center and finally Anaheim Plaza—was an immediate success.

An aggressive annexation policy over the years gobbled huge tracts of land, especially to the east, expanding the city from 4.3 square miles in 1954 to 42 square miles by the end of the 1970s.

Anaheim's first post-war tourist attrac-

Walt Disney started his career as a cartoonist in Kansas City after serving in World War I. Already famous for creating lovable Mickey Mouse and many other cartoon characters, Disney began to realize his lifelong dream of building an amusement park that the entire family could enjoy. After nearly 20 years of planning, ground was finally broken in 1954 to make way for the ever popular Disneyland in Anaheim. Courtesy, Anaheim Public Library

tion opened in 1952, called "Jungle Gardens." Owned by Jack Dutton, a future mayor of the city, Jungle Gardens featured Jerry, "the world's most human chimpanzee," and a menagerie of other exotic creatures, including birds, a pool of alligators, and an elephant named "Anaheim," all dwelling under more than 500 palms.

But it wasn't until a man named Walt Disney took a look at Anaheim that things really took off. Already famed for such animated classics as "Fantasia," and the creation of Mickey Mouse and other cartoon characters, Disney had dreamed since the 1930s of creating something different from the amusement parks of the day, which were dirty, sleazy, and no place for kids. He wanted a place that was clean, well run, and friendly enough for the whole family.

At first, Disney wanted the park on 18 acres he owned in Burbank, but the project needed more land than that. The Stanford Research Institute was commissioned to find a better site and in a 1953 report pinpointed the Anaheim area as best fitting Disney's criteria—including a central location, accessibility, and inexpensive land. After a long search, a 160-acre site south of Ball Road was chosen and purchased.

The ground was broken in July 1954, and the orange groves that made up most of the land were bulldozed down. A whole new world was sculpted in their place, with names like "Main Street USA," "Adventureland," and "Fantasyland." Walt Disney kept the nation updated about plans for his "Magic Kingdom" in his weekly television show; the excitement began to build.

Disneyland opened with a huge splash on July 17, 1955, with Bob Cummings, Art Linkletter, and Ronald Reagan hosting a coast-to-coast television event for 90 million television viewers, while 28,000 people gathered inside the park. They did not see perfection. The asphalt on Main Street USA had only been poured that morning and tugged at high-heeled shoes. A plumbers' strike had resulted in a dearth of drinking fountains, and many rides weren't working very well. But the new amusement park had captured people's imaginations and became an instant success, drawing its first million visitors in just seven weeks.

The Disney Hotel opened three months after the park, built by developer and Disney friend Jack Wrather. Just 100 rooms greeted guests then. Today the hotel has three high-rise towers and 1,174 rooms.

Disneyland's first major expansion came in 1959 with additions including the Matterhorn, a fleet of submarines, and the monorail. The latter, intended as a "train of the future," was the first passenger-carrying system of its kind in the Western

Hemisphere. To build it, Disneyland designers teamed with Germany's Alweg Company, which had developed an experimental monorail in Cologne.

The same year, Disneyland had its most famous non-visitor. Soviet Premier Nikita Khrushchev, on a visit to the United States, badly wanted to see the park, but was told that the logistics of security were impossible. Bitterly disappointed, he threw a tantrum, exclaiming, "Why not? What is it? Do you have rocket launching pads there? I do not know . . . For me, the situation is inconceivable; I cannot find the words to explain this to my people!"

Many world leaders, of course, did not share Khrushchev's problem, and they joined the celebrities and many millions of other guests who came to Disneyland from around the globe. Disneyland attracted so many foreign dignitaries in its early years that the *Christian Science Monitor* joked that it had become "almost an instrumentality of American foreign policy."

In the midst of the city's remarkable boom, Anaheim paused long enough to note a major milestone: the centennial of its founding in 1857. The 1957 celebration included a "Centurama," which depicted the history of Anaheim and featured a cast of 1,200. The hour-and-a-half production played for four nights at La Palma Park.

Taken just six weeks before the park's grand opening in 1955, this aerial photograph of Disneyland shows major construction still under way. Note the Main Street USA area in the foreground and Fantasyland with Sleeping Beauty's Castle in the background. Courtesy, Anaheim Public Library

Anaheim and Disneyland: A Happy Marriage

Few relationships between a city and a business have been as close and intertwined as that of Anaheim and Disneyland. Starting with Walt Disney's first interest in Anaheim as a possible site for his new type of amusement park, city officials knew what such a venture would do for Anaheim and bent over backwards to accommodate him. The only key figure who objected in the beginning was Mayor Pearson, who, when he heard of the plans, affirmed that he wanted no "honky-tonk" enterprise in Anaheim. In a personal meeting, Disney assured the mayor that his park would be a clean, wholesome place with no alcohol. Even shelled peanuts would not be sold to avoid their shucks being strewn across the park. Pearson was quickly converted and joined the all-out effort to find a place in Anaheim for Disneyland.

The task wasn't easy. Anaheim officials suffered with Disney as site after site proved unsuitable. One was too close to a rundown cemetery for Disney's liking. Another fell through when a real estate agent overheard City Administrator Murdock and Disney discussing it at a restaurant. The agent quickly bought up parcels in the area and offered land to Disney at an outrageous price, which was duly rejected. By 1954, six sites had been considered, then dropped.

Finally, 160 acres of orange groves south of Ball Road were chosen. This time, Murdock was determined that nothing was going to ruin the deal, not even the fact that Cerritos Avenue ran through the land. "After all this effort," Murdock said later, "we weren't going to let an arterial

highway stand in our way." The road was closed. Another problem was that the land lay outside of the city's boundaries. An annexation attempt might have jinxed the deal, since some of the site's occupants were opposed to joining the city. City officials carefully drew boundaries to exclude any opponents who might vote against annexation, and Disneyland was born.

Disneyland didn't transform Anaheim all by itself—the postwar boom was already bringing in many industries and tens of thousands of people—but its influence on Anaheim's development can hardly be overstated. Much of it was positive, such as the later construction of the Anaheim Convention Center and Anaheim Stadium, both close to the park and both, at least partially, made possible by it. But the park's presence was a mixed blessing. A "glitter gulch" of hotels quickly sprang up around the park, creating a place to stay for millions of tourists, but also creating a haven for prostitutes and crime.

The large hotel chains the city wanted were leery at first to build in Anaheim, where business dropped off after Disneyland's peak summer months. The city responded by building the convention center, ensuring a year-round business for the hotels. The center, and subsequent expansions, helped to attract the large hotel chains that began to locate in the city in the 1970s and 1980s.

Disneyland did more than bring people in from all over the world, it paved the way for more businesses and residents to locate there. It also fostered a style and philosophy that set the tone for the city, a tone that was unmistak-

ably Disney. That philosophy even had a name: The Anaheim Way. According to a booklet for employees at the convention center and Anaheim Stadium, the Anaheim Way meant:

There are no customers, only Guests! There are no workers or employees, only Hosts and Hostesses! Our Guests are the most important people in the world! . . . The most important word in our vocabulary is COURTESY! CLEANLINESS AND NEATNESS are our habits. SERVICE is our motto. We handle emergencies immediately. We resolve complaints in a friendly manner. We know the answers to questions! THE ANAHEIM WAY!

Grateful for what Disneyland had meant for the city, elected officials were often willing to bend over backward for the park. When an application was made in 1966 to build a tall hotel that would have looked down into Disneyland, park officials immediately objected, saying the hotel's presence would destroy the park's separation from the real world. The hotel was scratched, and the next year the city developed a "sight line" ensuring that no buildings outside of the park could be seen from the inside.

For the most part, city leaders and businessmen were happy to make such accommodations. After all, Disneyland was a major cause of the city's prosperity. In addition to the taxes it paid and the tourist dollars it brought, the park made Anaheim a city known throughout the world, and city leaders were grateful. Disneyland returned the favor by buying its goods and hiring its employees within the city as much as possible.

Other centennial activities included the planting of a time capsule in Anaheim City Park, guided tours of city landmarks, a shaving contest, a beard contest, and the selection of a queen.

By 1962, Anaheim's growth had made it the largest general-law city in the state, with between 125,000 and 130,000 residents. City officials began to feel limited by the general-law arrangement, which makes the state legislature the ultimate

proval from the state. Opponents argued that a charter could result in a "boss"-style government, with a strong mayor calling the shots and councilmen looking after the interests of his ward, not of the entire city. The concerns were answered by the committee, which opted against a ward system, kept the number of councilmen at five, and stayed with the city manager form of government. Anaheim voters approved the new charter on June 2, 1964. It was rati-

A landmark community institution, the Anaheim Public Library has been the recipient of many gifts, donations, collections, and historic memorabilia over the years. Here, artist "Pete" Mustard (left) presents a selection of his clown prints to Leo J. Friis (center) and William J. Griffith (right) at the library circa 1960. Courtesy, Anaheim Public Library

arbiter of city business. A committee was formed to draft a city charter, the municipal equivalent of a constitution, which essentially makes a city independent, limited only by the state and U.S. constitutions.

A 15-member Citizens Charter Study Committee worked on drafting a charter. Proponents argued that a charter would give the city more control and allow for better planning. For example, under the general-law setup, long-term financing needed ap-

fied by the state legislature early the next year. The charter has been amended several times. The biggest change came in 1974, when voters approved direct election of the mayor.

While the charter was being debated, the city council set into motion the development of a general plan for the city's growth, and established a four percent hotel room tax to help build a convention center, which city officials had dreamed of

Supporters of U.S. Senator nominee Thomas H. Kuchel kick off the campaign at Anaheim's Savoy Restaurant in 1954. Courtesy, Anaheim Public Library

for nearly a decade. Plans were unveiled for a $14.5-million Anaheim Convention Center in 1964. Built across from Disneyland's entrance on Katella Avenue, it was intended to give the city's summer-oriented tourist industry some year-round business. The huge convention center, with its space-age design, opened in July 1967, and more than 63,000 people attended shows and conventions its first year, a figure that would be dwarfed by the millions that would attend in later years.

After Disneyland and the convention center, a third jewel was added to the city's crown: Anaheim Stadium. The effort to bring major-league sports to Anaheim be-

gan in 1963, when Mayor Rex Coons dreamed of the benefits a sports complex could bring to the city. He knew just who could occupy it—baseball's Los Angeles Angels, then playing their home games in Dodger Stadium and not very happy about playing second fiddle to the more established Dodgers.

Serious talks began between the team's owners and the city the next year, but Anaheim almost lost the Angels when Long Beach intervened with a serious bid. But Long Beach made the fatal mistake of insisting that the team carry its name, while majority owner Gene Autry would accept no name but the California Angels. Coons

Pictured here under construction in the mid-1960s, the $14.5-million Anaheim Convention Center opened its doors in 1967, playing host to more than 63,000 visitors in the first year alone. Disneyland is visible to the upper right, just a short distance from the entrance of the Convention Center. Courtesy, Anaheim Public Library

told Autry he could call the team anything he wanted. The Angels then agreed to come to Anaheim, as long as a stadium was ready for them by April 1966.

That was only two years away, not much time to build a major stadium. The facility was supposed to be a joint project between the city and the county of Orange, making the total price tag of $21 million more manageable. When the county board of supervisors backed out at the last minute— believing the venture was too risky— Anaheim officials forged ahead anyway. The city council created a separate non-profit corporation to build the stadium and lease it back to the city, which also avoided the risky and time-consuming problem of a public vote.

Construction began immediately on nearly 150 acres of vacant land bought from real estate broker C.J. Gill. Nearly 8,000 tons of steel, 1,900 lights, and 43,204 seats went into the construction. The stadium, completed for $15.8 million, was formally inaugurated on April 9, 1966, in an exhibition game with the San

Francisco Giants that drew 40,735 fans. Later, on July 11, 1967, Anaheim hosted the Major League All-Star Game. As 46,309 watched, the National League prevailed in a 2-1 game that went a record-breaking 15 innings.

But the stadium needed more than baseball to be profitable, and it was losing money every year. As city officials sought a professional football team to help fill the gaps between baseball seasons, other events were tried, including rock and roll. Rock concerts sometimes left an unexpected weeding job for the city; dozens of marijuana plants sprouted afterwards in the outfield, apparently seeded by the leftover butts of marijuana cigarettes.

The city made up the stadium's losses in profits from its electrical utility. The city-run electric utility often played a major, if largely unsung, role in helping to finance major projects. In buying electric power wholesale from Southern California Edison and selling it to residents and businesses at rates slightly

RIGHT: President, majority owner, and chairman of the board of the Los Angeles Angels (known today as the California Angels), world-renowned entertainer Gene Autry played a crucial role in moving his team to Anaheim upon completion of the Anaheim Stadium in 1966. Courtesy, Anaheim Public Library

cheaper than those in other cities, Anaheim enticed industries to relocate for the lower rates. The utility was also able to raise emergency money for city projects through occasional rate increases. The practice ended in 1978 with a city amendment that limited profits from the utility.

In 1978, the city approached the Los Angeles Rams, a football team that happened to be unhappy with its home in the Los Angeles Memorial Coliseum. Anaheim offered to expand Anaheim Stadium

to the tune of $33 million, and also agreed to allow the Rams ownership to build on a portion of the stadium parking lot. Once again, the city didn't let pride get in the way, as Anaheim permitted the team to keep Los Angeles in its name. The stadium was enlarged by 27,000 seats by April 1980, and the Rams played their first game there on August 11. The stadium was finally a money-maker.

As the new Anaheim emerged, pieces of old Anaheim were gradually falling away. The Valencia

Completed in 1966 by the Del E. Webb Company, the $15.8-million Anaheim Stadium was built on nearly 150 acres of land, using some 8,000 tons of steel. The A-frame scoreboard that rises 230 feet into the air is the source of the stadium's nickname, the "Big-A." In addition to hosting the California Angels, the Anaheim Stadium is now home to the Los Angeles Rams. Courtesy, Anaheim Public Library

orange industry was already reeling from the effects of "quick decline," and many of the trees bulldozed in the name of progress had been already dying of the disease. Valencia groves throughout Orange County disappeared as the building boom spread, leaving only about 20,000 acres by the 1960s. Oranges would remain a part of the future of Anaheim and the rest of Orange County, but were never again as important to the city.

The amazing growth also filled the city's schools and created the need for new ones. After Western High School opened in 1957, Anaheim Union High School dropped the "union" from its name.

How did a sleepy agricultural town with less than 15,000 residents in 1950 suddenly blossom into a city that in only two decades saw the arrival of Disneyland, the largest convention center west of the Mississippi, and two major sports franchises and, in the process, grew to a total of 166,701 residents by 1970? Some of it, of course, was luck, including a freeway that plowed right through the middle of town, thousands of returning veterans, and cheap land that attracted major employers. But without planning, aggressive campaigns to attract business and industry, and the willingness to take financial risks, many of Anaheim's successes would have gone elsewhere. In the early 1970s, Mayor Jack Dutton offered a mostly facetious explanation of how Anaheim had accomplished what it had:

People often ask us how we do it. They want to know how a town with such a small permanent population can build huge, nationally known, professionally run and staffed facilities like the convention center and Anaheim Stadium, and I always tell them that we are primarily old-timers here with our roots deep in the agricultural traditions, and maybe we are just so dumb we don't know we shouldn't be able to do these things!

Anaheim's wildest dreams had come true. But success always has a price. In Anaheim's case, the most costly side effect was a downtown that steadily deteriorated. The older commercial and residential sections north of the Santa Ana Freeway were the victims of success, first of Anaheim Center, which drew away many customers; then of Disneyland and the Anaheim Convention Center, around which developed new businesses that housed and provided shopping for the city's tourist and convention crowds.

Reviving a decrepit downtown became the next goal for city leaders, who continued to dream of ways to make Anaheim even better—only this time, it was going to be a little more difficult to make dreams come true.

Anaheim's burgeoning growth created the need for new schools in the 1950s and 1960s, such as the Western High School, which was established in 1957. Here, Western High students celebrate the holidays with a presentation of a living Christmas tree in the 1970s. Courtesy, Anaheim Public Library

While Anaheim moves towards the future, it does not forget its past. The creation of Heritage Square is a praiseworthy restoration effort, helping to preserve Anaheim's exciting and compelling history. The area will contain five historic buildings when completed, including the Ferdinand Backs home, which was constructed in 1904. Courtesy, Anaheim Bulletin

A New Beginning

The history of Anaheim is filled with dreamers: the San Franciscan musicians John Frohling and Charles Kohler,who sought to create a vineyard colony on land that a ranchero thought "not fit for a goat"; the inexperienced vinters who battled adversity to make Anaheim the largest wine-producing center in the state; the merchants who tried to make the city an industrial center in the 1920s; the citrus farmers who made the area the Valencia capital of the world; the civic leaders who foresaw the explosive growth after World War II and made sure Anaheim was ready for it; and Walt Disney, who transformed a 160-acre plot of orange groves into a new kind of amusement park that would put Anaheim on the map and set the stage for a huge convention center and major-league sports.

Of course, dreams don't always come true or last. The thriving vineyard colony was destroyed by a tiny parasite no one discovered for six decades. The plans to make Anaheim an industrial giant were deferred first by the invasion of the Ku Klux Klan, then by the Great Depression, and again by World War II. The citrus industry boomed for decades, but eventually fell to a combination of quick decline and bulldozers. Even the lasting triumphs had unintended side effects, such as the "glitter gulch" of hotels near Disneyland that too often attracted prostitution and other crime, and a downtown that steadily declined as customers went elsewhere.

Still, as Anaheim entered the 1970s, the city was in remarkably good shape. With healthy revenues from tourism, conventions, sales taxes, and other sources, Ana-

heim ranked first in the state in creating its own resources. Its industrial areas were the fastest growing in the nation. Disneyland and the convention center continued to attract millions every year. The Angels were in town, and by the end of the decade the Rams would make Anaheim Stadium a profitable operation.

But now the city had to do something about its downtown. Numerous proposals were made over the years, including one in the 1960s that would have made the area a business and recreation center, complete with a 15-acre lake in the middle. Another would have given the area an international flavor similar to that of Solvang, central California's Danish-style city. Yet another idea was the "Avenue of Flags," which would have dressed up Lincoln Avenue with the banner of every nation and every state in the union. Finally, feeling they had to start largely from scratch to revitalize downtown, city officials came up with an answer: redevelopment.

The city's Redevelopment Agency, with its reins in the hands of the city council, began operating in 1973. Soon after came the approval of the first phase, called Project Alpha. Named for the first letter in the alphabet, Project Alpha included 200 acres of downtown Anaheim and 2,366 acres in the city's industrial zone, later increased to 3,096. A 634-acre section of Anaheim Hills was also in the original plans, but later was dropped when that area prospered without help.

In the early years, Project Alpha was very active. Traffic patterns were reconstructed to enable Lincoln Avenue, Anaheim Boulevard, and Harbor Boulevard to

The chamber of commerce building, completed in 1984, cost $3 million to construct and now gives the city of Anaheim a contemporary image and a new modern look. Photo by Larry Molmud

handle more traffic. Hundreds of downtown buildings on two dozen city blocks were demolished.

But as the demolition of downtown continued—much of it through the use of eminent domain—criticism grew against Project Alpha. Disagreements developed over the future direction of the project, and plans were stalled as most of the land where buildings had been demolished lay vacant for more than a decade.

When the follow-up to Project Alpha, Project Beta, was unveiled by city officials in 1975, angry residents fought it vigorously. The proposal, intended to improve a 2,755-acre area south of Alpha and east of Disneyland, was finally abandoned.

In the meantime, Project Alpha began tackling an urgent need for the city: a new city hall. Despite the city's enormous growth, it had continued to rely on its aging Greek-style city hall, built in 1923. By the early 1970s, 86 city employees were packed into a space intended for 50, and 1,400 other employees were scattered in more than a dozen other locations around the city.

Despite the desperate need for a new city hall, local voters were not enamored with the proposals that emerged to build one. They rejected a $3-million bond in 1963, an $8-million bond in 1970, and even a lease-back plan in 1974 that would have cleared the way for the sale of revenue bonds to build a new civic center.

City officials decided to avoid another vote and pay for a new city hall from a combination of sources, eventually including redevelopment money, revenue-sharing funds, the sale of city land, and utility profits. The groundbreaking for the new seven-story Anaheim Civic Center on Anaheim Boulevard came on March 1, 1978. As the $14-million structure was dedicated in day-long festivities on June 24, 1980, about 2,000 people came by to inspect the new facility—about the same number that helped to dedicate the old city hall 57 years before. That building was torn down to make room for a parking structure and the new $3-million chamber of commerce office building, completed in 1984.

But criticism of redevelopment was building and finally hit a crescendo in 1987, when the city began pushing its new Project Katella. The project focused on 4,387 acres surrounding and between Disneyland and Anaheim Stadium. Though city officials insisted no structures would be torn down, residents fought the plan and formed Anaheim H.O.M.E. (Homeowners

LEFT: Known for his Carl's Jr., enterprise, Carl Karcher is also an active participant in Anaheim community affairs. Courtesy, Anaheim Public Library

The redevelopment boom of the 1970s and 1980s gave rise to intensive construction and a revitalized downtown district. Courtesy, Anaheim Bulletin

The transformation of Santa Ana Canyon into the affluent Anaheim Hills development began in 1971, and by the early 1980s, more than 15,000 people had moved into 2,700 new luxury homes. Courtesy, City of Anaheim, Public Information Office

Stunning snow-capped mountains provide a breathtaking backdrop for the Anaheim Hills Golf and Country Club. Courtesy, Anaheim Bulletin

term, positive side of redevelopment, focusing only on the demolition and the vacant lots.

Some of the victims of redevelopment have been buildings considered important to the city's history, including the Pickwick Hotel, the SQR store, and the Anaheim Fox Theatre. However, efforts were made to preserve the past, including the creation of Heritage Square, a preservation area that will include five historic buildings when it is completed, including the Ferdinand Backs home, completed in 1904. Redevelopment has also left the 1908 Carnegie library intact—it is now the Anaheim Museum—and the Kraemer building, built in 1925.

As the 1980s ended, the city's dreams for Project Alpha finally seemed destined to come true, as relations with citizens groups improved and firm plans were developed. A 16-acre business and commercial development called Anaheim Center was approved in January 1990.

One symptom of downtown Anaheim's troubles was the decline of the Halloween Festival, which had been a major

for Maintaining their Environment). Its efforts helped pack one redevelopment meeting with 1,700 angry residents. Project Katella was defeated.

Other citizens groups emerged to fight different aspects of the city's redevelopment, including the Anaheim Neighborhood Association and the West Anaheim Political Action Committee.

City officials claimed that opposing resident groups refused to see the long-

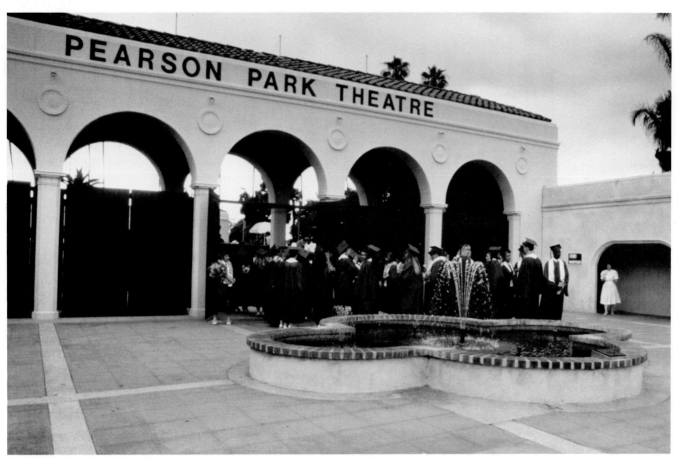

social event in the city since 1924. The festival's sponsor of so many years, the chamber of commerce, bowed out in 1976, saying it could no longer afford to put on the event. A committee of local businessmen handled the festival for two years. Then another group headed by local industrialist Herb Leo and representatives from Disneyland and the Bank of America took over in 1978 with help from a city grant. Finally, a nonprofit corporation was formed to organize the event, relying on help from local service clubs. The event was renamed the Orange County Fall Festival to reflect its countywide appeal, and remains a popular event.

Many place much of the blame for downtown's initial woes on Anaheim Plaza, the county's first shopping mall, which had begun with a Broadway department store in 1955. Known as Anaheim Center in the early years, it began as a great success, though it drew many customers away from the older downtown. As the years passed, however, it began to suffer from competition from newer malls, as well as its poor freeway access, despite its proximity to the Santa Ana Freeway. It was enclosed, completely remodeled, and renamed Anaheim Plaza in 1973, but its problems continued. The city plans to redevelop the center and the surrounding area in the 1990s.

The city's older residential areas in the western "flatlands" are marked by tract housing. The 1970s and 1980s saw the affluent addition of Anaheim Hills, a rustic area formerly known as Santa Ana Canyon. The city annexed the 4,200-acre cattle ranch owned by Louis E. Nohl. Texaco Ventures Inc. and Anaheim Hills Inc. purchased the land in 1971 and began its transformation. By the early 1980s, more than 15,000 people had

Named in honor of long-time mayor Charles Pearson, the popular Pearson Park features an outdoor Greek Theatre, which is host to many cultural and educational activities, including this graduation ceremony. Photo by Bo Richards

ABOVE: Children of all ages continue to delight in the charm and adventure of Disneyland. Courtesy, Walt Disney Productions

FACING PAGE: The rural surroundings of the luxurious Anaheim Hills development provide for scenic getaways in the heart of the city. Courtesy, Anaheim Bulletin

moved into a total of 2,700 homes, many of them costing more than a million dollars, prompting one magazine article to marvel, "Anaheim actually has two Magic Kingdoms: the one Walt Disney built off Harbor Boulevard and the one gradually creeping through the canyons and over the hilltops towards the city's eastern border."

The eastward expansion has continued, as Anaheim annexed the Bauer, Wallace, and Oak Hills ranches in the mid-1980s, adding another 1,300 acres to the city. The city created special tax districts in the new developments to help pay for the enormous costs of extending roads, schools, police, and other public services. In the future, Anaheim hopes to expand ever eastward to the Riverside County border. By the year 2000, the population of Anaheim Hills is expected to reach 65,000.

Even a growing and bustling city needs culture. One way citizens ensured there was a place for the arts in Anaheim was through the creation of the Anaheim Cultural Arts Center. After Horace Mann Elementary School closed in 1969 because of earthquake safety standards, a grassroots effort persuaded the Anaheim Elementary School District to lease it to a citizens group at no cost two years later. After much remodeling, it reopened on June 9, 1973, and became the showcase for a wide range of cultural activities, including ballet, arts and crafts, sketching, needlework, drama, and gymnastics. Leased by the Anaheim Foundation for Culture and the Arts, the center has become a home to many arts groups, including the Orange County Black Actors Theater, the Ana-Modjeska Players, the Patrick Gaza Ballet Company, the

ABOVE: The Anaheim Convention Center was part of a general plan to accommodate the city's tourism trade in the early 1960s. The dome-shaped convention center opened its doors in July 1967, with more than 63,000 people attending varied events throughout the first year. Photo by Larry Molmud

RIGHT AND FACING PAGE: Anaheim's elegant historic buildings and glass-adorned office towers help to create a striking architectural blend of the city's past, present, and future. The seven-story Anaheim Civic Center (facing page) was dedicated in 1980, and the charming Heritage Square (right) is currently under development. Photo of Heritage Square by Bo Richards. Photo of Anaheim Civic Center courtesy, Anaheim Bulletin

FACING PAGE, TOP: A jubilant Anaheim High School senior celebrates her graduation. Courtesy, Anaheim Bulletin

FACING PAGE, BOTTOM: Carl Anderson takes some licks from his German Shepherd, Heidi, while restoring his 1940 Packard Coupe at his home in Anaheim. Photo by Ken Steinhardt

ABOVE: A major entertainment and active sports capital, Anaheim is also a place filled with small-town charm in which families can live, work, and play. Photo by Ken Steinhardt

LEFT: This police officer takes a moment to play with neighborhood children while on foot patrol through a local Anaheim community. Courtesy, Anaheim Bulletin

*Anaheim's many parks
and playgrounds offer a
fun and adventurous at-
mosphere for the area's children. Courtesy, Anaheim
Bulletin*

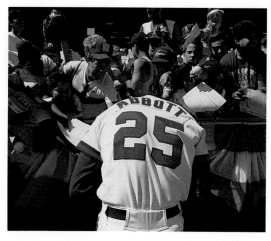

ABOVE: Honored on TOPPS' All-Star Rookie Team in 1989, pitcher James Abbott is one of the California Angels' youngest and most promising players. Courtesy, Anaheim Bulletin

LEFT: Summer in Anaheim is a time of playful recreation and cool refreshment. Courtesy, Anaheim Bulletin

LEFT: Charming homes with elegant architectural details can be found throughout the city of Anaheim. Pictured here in the den of their home on a late afternoon are Leslie and Bill Koon. Their house still features the original hardwood floors that were first installed in 1924. Photo by Ken Steinhardt

Anaheim Art Association, and the Cathleen Forcucci Dance Academy.

The city's first park, developed in 1921, was renamed Pearson Park in 1960, a year after longtime Mayor Charles Pearson retired. The popular park underwent major refurbishing in the mid-1980s, including a rebuilding of the bleachers exactly as they had been in 1927, down to the wooden roof and Spanish-style painting along the walls. The outdoor Greek Theatre, built in 1927 and renamed after Pearson in 1975, also was refurbished.

The 1980s saw several major disasters in Anaheim, including a devastating firestorm on April 22, 1982. Fanned by Santa Ana winds, the fire swept through 50 apartment buildings and left 1,500 people homeless, but resulted in an outpouring of help from other residents and the American Red Cross, including food, money, and temporary housing. The fire spurred local ordinances throughout the county restricting the use of wood shake roofs. On June 22, 1985, a fire at the Larry Fricker Co. plant, which manufactured herbicides and pesticides, forced a three-day evacuation of 7,500 people living nearby.

In 1983, part of the agreement that brought the Rams to Anaheim (permitting the football team's owners to build on a portion of the stadium parking) prompted the Angels to file a $400 million lawsuit against the city. The Angels contended that the planned 1.7-million-square-foot office and retail complex would do away with too much of the stadium's parking. In 1988, an Orange County Superior Court judge ruled that the development should be permitted, as long as the Angels are guaranteed more than 12,000 outdoor parking spaces. Still, both sides asked for a clarification of the ruling, and as the 1980s drew to a close, the outcome was still in doubt.

Both the Angels and the Rams gave Anaheim winning teams in the 1980s, though world championships eluded both organizations. The Rams made it to the Super Bowl in 1980, only to lose to the Pittsburgh Steelers. The Angels won division championships in 1982 and 1986, but missed making it to the World Series—though they came within one pitch of it in 1986. On July 11, 1989, Angel Stadium was again the scene for the Major League All-Star Game, bringing more national attention to the city and to Orange County, which used the game as one of several events celebrating its centennial that year.

Anaheim also earned a bit of Olympic glory in the 1984 games in Los Angeles, first from the Olympic torch run that filled the streets with thousands of people as it was passed through the city, and later with the wrestling competition held at the Anaheim Convention Center. More significant to the city was an unprecedented hotel building boom spurred by anticipation of Olympic visitors. The newcomers included the 1,600-room Anaheim Hilton and Towers, the largest in the state, which opened in May 1984. By the end of the decade, the city had a total of 159 hotels and motels and a staggering 18,000 total hotel rooms; a far cry from the day Disneyland opened, when there were five hotels and two motels with a total of 87 rooms.

In the mid-1980s, city officials began to look into the possibility of bringing yet another major sports franchise into Anaheim. After the city of Santa Ana failed in an effort with Westdome Partnership to attract a professional basketball team there, Anaheim signed a tentative agreement in 1986 with Westdome to build an arena for basketball and other events. The plans fell through as efforts to attract a team failed again, but the dream of a third sports franchise wasn't finished yet. As the 1990s began, Anaheim and Santa Ana both were planning to build arenas, each hoping to eventually entice a basketball team.

The city's industrial growth contin-

FACING PAGE: The Central City Neighborhood Council was formed in an effort to maintain the community in the fight against rampant development. Photo by Ken Steinhardt

ued, though not as feverishly as in the 1950s and 1960s. By 1987 there were 500 industries in Anaheim, and a total employment in the city of 149,000. Today, the city boasts many of the biggest employers in Orange County, including Rockwell International, Northrop Corporation, Pacific Bell, Disneyland, and Carl Karcher Enterprises. By the late 1980s, the city had more than 500 industries, and a total employment of more than 150,000.

The Anaheim Convention Center continued to grow, with two major expansions in 1974 and 1982, bringing its total square footage to 685,000 by the end of the decade and accommodating 1.6 million people who attend events there every year. The largest convention facility on the West Coast, the center underwent its first major facelift in late 1989. The $10-million remodeling was accompanied by a $30-million expansion that was to bring the center's total square footage to 835,000 by mid-1990.

Disneyland expanded and improved its attractions over the years. Space Mountain was added in 1977, Big Thunder in 1979, a refurbished Fantasyland in 1983, and Splash Mountain in 1989. Also in 1989, the park honored its 300 millionth guest.

But even Disneyland could not be totally immune from the world's problems. The park was hit by a 22-day strike in 1984 when more than 1,800 employees refused to accept a two-year freeze on wages and cuts in fringe benefits.

Prostitution became such a major problem in the city that in the early 1980s the county courts set bail for Anaheim prostitutes at $5,000, while the bail was set at $1,000 for those from other cities.

The four freeways plying their way through Anaheim played a major role in bringing growth to the city, but in the 1980s grew increasingly clogged. Traffic became a countywide issue, as voters rejected sales tax increases in 1984 and 1989 that would have funded transportation projects. In Anaheim, voters turned down a 1988 proposal to sell bonds to improve 33 crucial intersections.

Housing costs were another regional worry, with Orange County's housing stock among the most expensive in the nation. Business leaders fretted that as workers found the area too expensive, the shortage

of labor would prompt some businesses to leave the city for more affordable areas. By the end of 1989, the median price of a home in Orange County was more than $222,000.

As the 1980s ended, it was clear many residents still dreamed of a better Anaheim. As a way of making some of those dreams come true in 1986 the city launched Vision 2000, a "strategic planning process for the community of Anaheim," intended to bring the city into the twenty-first century. Citizen committees drew up recommendations, which were approved by the city council in early 1987. The goals were further refined during two more years of meetings, public hearings, and many hours of planning effort.

Transportation emerged as the biggest issue needing solutions, with proposals that included completing a program to synchronize traffic signals, improve freeways, encourage carpooling, and widen 28 busy intersections. The report also urged better city leadership by allowing more citizen input and starting training programs for newly elected council members. A wide range of recommendations was also given for preserving older neighborhoods, enforcing drug laws more effectively, and improving police and fire protection.

The idea of linking the city and other parts of Orange County with a monorail has been dreamed of since Walt Disney built his, and could eventually become reality. So could a plan to link Anaheim and Las Vegas with a 250-mph train that would put the two cities only 70 minutes apart.

Despite overwhelming growth and change, Anaheim has managed to preserve much of its history. In addition to the old homes to be showcased at Heritage Square, a stately, three-story 1894 Victorian serves as an office for the American Red Cross on West Street, built by

German immigrant John Woelke. But next to it, almost hidden by trees and plain by comparison, is the city's most historic structure: the Mother Colony House, erected for George Hansen and the first building of the vintner colony that launched the city in the late 1850s. Moved from its original spot at the northeast corner of today's Lincoln Avenue and Anaheim Boulevard to 414 N. West Street, it is also the oldest museum in Orange County, having served the city in that function since 1929. And tucked inside a small shopping center on 6398 E. Santa Ana Canyon Road is the Ramon

Longtime residents of Anaheim, Rosa Togel (left) and her sister Hertha MacLachlan (right) grew up in their North Zeyn Street home. Rosa has lived in the family house since 1928. Photo by Ken Steinhardt

Peralta adobe, built in 1871.

Anaheim's early colonists surely could not have foreseen the city that had emerged 130 years later—a city that stretched 26 miles from east to west, with 45 square miles and a population of 244,000 in between. They could not have foreseen an Anaheim that had become a major sports and entertainment capital visited by millions annually. Much of that was achieved through planning and vision—vision that, its residents hope, can tackle any problems that emerge over the next decade and bring Anaheim into the twenty-first century stronger than ever.

*One of Orange County's fledgling social organiza-
tions, the Woodmen of the World, was established in
1890 as a fraternal aid society. Pictured here in this
1898 portrait are members of the Anaheim chapter
in full ceremonial robes, holding the organization's
symbolic axes. Courtesy, Anaheim Public Library*

Partners In Progress

If Anaheim's German colonists visited the city today, they might show surprise at its sheer size and population numbers. But they would feel right at home in Anaheim's vigorous business community and its energetic and diverse approach to success—qualities that the early leaders practiced heartily.

Consider the modern-day diversity—from construction firms to aerospace support to restaurants and health care. Growth figures of these organizations speak for the wisdom of leaders who helped create an economic climate in which to prosper.

Among Anaheim's most notable success stories is business pioneer Carl Karcher, who gave Anaheim his vote of confidence more than 50 years ago. Today Karcher's restaurants provide good food and old-fashioned service on an international basis.

Kwikset Corporation is another familiar Anaheim name, dating from the pre-boom era when industries were just beginning to move to Orange County's hub. Kwikset is now known as an industry leader in hardware and security products.

The pivotal years after World War II, which drew many veterans to California, were establishing dates for a number of Anaheim's businesses, especially defense and aerospace industries and their supporting goods and services. Today's business support services are as sophisticated as the information-age and space-age clients they serve.

Perhaps the history of Yellow Cab is one of the most representative of Anaheim's growth. Company services grew from the original taxi concept to rapid transit diversification, shopping center shuttles, and special group transportation.

Second- and third-generation family businesses are commonplace in Anaheim, too, especially in the construction and building trades. Small family firms that started out building the much-needed postwar housing ("Everyone needed a house then," says one business owner) often grew to fuel commercial and industrial building construction as well.

That boom, in turn, led to the need for furnishings, decorating, landscaping, and pool and recreation equipment, to name only a few of the ancillary industries that flourished with the population in Anaheim and the surrounding communities.

Anaheim has been exemplary in the human services category as well, providing medical management, mobile medical clinics, and industrial and sports medicine. Its hospitals have evolved from small community units to large health care systems, often with extensive networks of resources and capabilities.

Some people attribute their success in Anaheim to hard work; others cite good luck and timing. No matter what, the organizations that appear on the following pages, who have chosen to participate in this important literary and civic project, have found their winning combination.

ANAHEIM CHAMBER OF COMMERCE

ABOVE: The Anaheim Chamber of Commerce building is located at 100 South Anaheim Boulevard.

RIGHT: The Anaheim Chamber of Commerce has been serving the business community since the turn of the century. Photo courtesy Anaheim Public Library

Celebrity is an integral part of Anaheim, home to Disneyland, baseball's California Angels, and football's Los Angeles Rams. Yet its solid business core extends well beyond sports and entertainment.

"Our famous residents have given Anaheim high name recognition around the United States and abroad," notes Allan B. Hughes, executive director of the Anaheim Chamber of Commerce. "We don't have to introduce ourselves to people in Kansas City or Tokyo or London, because we are already known. But we do emphasize our diverse range of opportunities in industrial and retail sectors, as well as our tourist and convention trade."

Certainly the community benefits from prominent sports and entertainment figures who give freely of their time, going to schools or civic groups to tout worthy causes. That spirit of volunteerism and vitality is commonplace in the community.

Hughes describes the chamber as a highly effective, well-rounded group, recognized by top executives in the area as one of quality and professionalism. Its successful programs and outstanding leadership have garnered recognition over the years from the United States Chamber of Commerce.

Among the Anaheim chamber's strengths are effective organization within its volunteer ranks, objective evaluation of the community's needs, responsible planning, and strong support of free enterprise and community self-reliance.

The chamber was established in 1895 to play a vital role in Anaheim's development. It reflected the pioneering spirit of the times, and it grew in stature along with the community. As a voluntary organization with a small executive staff of nine people, it offers unity to its varied business and professional membership of more than 1,300 organizations, spread around a broad geographical area. Notably its two dozen active committees and subcommittees offer guidance and support to business ventures of all types and sizes.

The chamber was first accredited by the U.S. parent organization in 1972, and received its 15-year reaccreditation in 1986. At that time the chamber was recognized as one of the top 10 in the United States.

In 1984 the chamber began a new chapter in its history by dedicating a newly constructed headquarters building. Located at 100 South Anaheim Boulevard, the chamber's quarters overlook the Civic Center Plaza, just north of city hall at the heart of the revitalized downtown area.

In breaking new ground for the 1990s, the chamber is becoming increasingly active in local, state, and national affairs and legislation. Through its strategic planning committee, the chamber works with the City of Anaheim to encourage visitors and businesses to locate there. The chamber is also an information source for visitors and newcomers and an education and networking source for its members. Through its new programs the Anaheim Chamber of Commerce is a progressive—and aggressive—force within the city.

DuBOIS TOWING

When the first DuBois Garage opened in Anaheim in 1929, motor vehicles were still a luxury. There were no freeways and no gridlock. Times were simpler then.

Times have changed, of course. Today DuBois Towing serves one of the busiest traffic areas in the nation. When the late Henry J. DuBois started his business—a business that has kept his name throughout its more than 60-year history—he had one tow truck. It was homemade; it was a modified pickup truck that held towing equipment. His business was open 24 hours a day, seven days a week,

For 60 years DuBois Towing has served Orange County's highways and byways.

and his drivers were also mechanics who often pulled disabled vehicles out of the abundant orange groves.

In 1946 DuBois took a partner, Bud Paschall, and as DuBois & Paschall the company expanded to three trucks, still offering 24-hour garage and towing services. They sold the business in 1962 to Duane J. Cahoon, now deceased, who operated it as a garage and body shop. When Cahoon retired in 1975 the

business reverted to the founder's son, Richard J. DuBois, and two partners, Mil Schaible and Richard C. Boggs. The threesome shared their corporation until 1986, when Boggs became sole owner.

Boggs closed the garage and body shop to concentrate on towing service in northern Orange County for the local police department, the California Highway Patrol, commercial accounts, and three major auto clubs: National Automobile, Amoco Motor, and Allstate Motor clubs.

Over the years DuBois changed locations, but it has always been downtown. From North Lemon Street to 113 West Chestnut (in 1942), in 1980 the company moved to its present location at 500 South Atchison Street near the Anaheim Civic Center. There is room to store more than 120 vehicles at a time, both indoors and out.

Boggs began working for DuBois & Paschall in 1965, and he learned the business from entry level up. A former U.S. Marine, he moved to California after he left the service.

He is owner and general manager of the family business. His wife, Fay, is office manager, and his daughter, Sara, is also involved in the business.

"Our work is a challenge because we don't always meet people on their best behavior," Richard Boggs notes. "When you are having car trouble or trying to retrieve a car that has been towed, you want to get mad at somebody. It's fascinating to see how people react under pressure."

Moving the vehicles has become more of a science, too, with plastic, rubber, and fiberglass parts involved. It requires more precision to avoid damaging the vehicle. In fact, all DuBois Towing drivers must take a special course to do the job right. Boggs explains, "We spend a lot of time with our drivers to instill spirit and pride in their work. We want them to treat each car as if it were their own."

McMAHAN BUSINESS INTERIORS

McMahan Desk Incorporated was established in 1967 by the late Jay McMahan. Originally McMahan Desk supplied economy-priced metal desks, chairs, filing cabinets, and used furniture to local businesses that were primarily concerned with function. As the demand grew, higher quality products were added, including executive furniture, open office systems, and custom furnishings.

The showroom is currently located at 1960 South Anaheim Boulevard, one block south of its original location. Four generations of the McMahan family have worked to develop the family business. Present owner Shirley McMahan currently oversees the company with her three sons, Marty, Jeff, and Alan Schlom. In addition, their younger sister, Shari McMahan, works as an environmental consultant.

In 1983 McMahan Desk established a space-planning and design department to better service its clients.

McMahan's 15,000-square-foot showroom displays a wide variety of office furnishings and systems.

"We are gradually using McMahan Business Interiors as our name because it reflects the company's broader scope," says president Marty Schlom. The design staff offers full-service space planning and interior design to its clients. Although the primary emphasis is with businesses located in Southern California, the firm is staffed to handle projects and installations nationwide.

"There is a direct correlation between office environments and employee morale," states Caren Ureda, director of design. Important elements, including a well-planned work environment, correct lighting, proper seating, and color-coordinated finishes and materials are all designed to enhance employee efficiency and productivity. Recent research has demonstrated the importance of ergonomic seating, designed to provide

maximum lumbar and leg support and correct body-weight distribution. Fatigue associated with long hours at the computer can be prevented with proper seating and good posture.

Clients benefit from the product lines and services offered by McMahan. The company's 15,000-square-foot showroom displays a wide range of office furnishings and systems—both contemporary and traditional styles. In addition, its adjacent warehouse stocks a significant quantity of products. McMahan's fleet of trucks, experienced furniture installers, and service technicians help provide efficiency in distribution.

Although McMahan Business Interiors caters to commercial, industrial, and high-technology firms, as well as county and city government agencies, it provides market knowledge, quality service, product excellence, and professionalism to all its clients in developing and maintaining long-term relationships.

HOYE, GRAVES, BAILEY, ACCOUNTANTS

The well-established certified public accounting firm of Hoye, Graves, Bailey, Accountants, has deep roots in the Anaheim area, but it is in fact an offshoot of a firm in the eastern United States.

In 1946, in Washington, D.C., the late Schell Hoye established the practice that still carries his name. He was joined 10 years later by William E.B. Graves, who is still with the firm there. George Bailey came on board in 1951, though he did not

California to work for a national accounting firm, then for a private company. He soon realized his preference for public accounting.

"The solution was simple," Bailey recalls. "Hoye, Graves wanted to set up an office in California, and I wanted to work with them again." So the West Coast office opened in August 1961 at its first Anaheim location, 1055 North Harbor.

Simultaneously, Bailey bought out an existing practice to augment

rejoined Hoye, Graves, Bailey three years later.

The firm's primary business includes audits, individual and corporate tax returns, and business services, such as bookkeeping, payroll, personnel screening of accountant applicants, and general advisory. As generalists for year-round accounts, the firm's staff serves local industries of all types, from trucking and construction to printing and real estate.

Today's Anaheim headquarters

become a partner until 1961, when he opened the California office.

Bailey first learned of Schell Hoye and his practice in the nation's capital through a mutual friend. Bailey was himself an easterner, born in New Jersey and raised in Rochester, New York. After he graduated from Syracuse University with a degree in business administration, Bailey was lured by the aura of Washington, D.C., and he took his certified public accountant test there.

The 1950s turned out to be a busy decade for Bailey. A World War II veteran, he was recalled for service in Korea. Afterward he went to

the firm's West Coast start. Bailey hired CPA Robert L. Johnson, Jr., an Anaheim native, in 1969. Today Johnson is principal owner as Bailey nears retirement.

A graduate of Anaheim High School in 1963, Fullerton College, and California State University, Long Beach, Johnson—like Bailey—reached a point where he wanted to try his hand at corporate accounting.

"In 1976 I left the company to join the staff of a corporation listed on the New York Stock Exchange," Johnson says. "I too found out that I'm much more interested in public accounting, with its diversity." He

The staff of Hoye, Graves, Bailey, Accountants: (left to right) George K. Bailey, Kathlene N. Rosenberger, Harold Cosby, Evelyn J. Beigh, Robert L. Johnson, Jr., and Shari L. Palmer.

at 1126 North Brookhurst is home to a staff of six people (the shortest employee tenure is 10 years) and a comprehensive computerized system.

"Hoye, Graves, Bailey, Accountants, has worked with some of its clients for more than 25 years," says Johnson.

"Our personal relationship with our clients is important. It is that longevity in serving them that makes us feel like a part of their business."

LA HABRA PRODUCTS, INC.

Chuck Kingsland, son of the founder of La Habra Products, is shown with a hand truck used in the mid-1940s. Forklifts were not in common use until the 1960s.

Known by its slogan of "The Finishing Touch Since 1926," La Habra Products' primary building material—stucco—is synonymous with the California life-style.

The Anaheim-based company, owned and operated as a third-generation family business, produces an extensive product line of building materials that includes exterior color coating, fiber-reinforced wall plaster, textured coverings, and a number of other industry staples.

The company was founded in 1926 by Nathan Kingsland, grandfather of the firm's current president Tod Kingsland, to manufacture pre-mixed stucco. The original company supplied markets in Burbank and Alhambra.

When Walt Disney announced his intent to build the Magic Kingdom in Anaheim, La Habra management bought two acres of land nearby, then covered with orange groves, in anticipation of the area's growth. Gradually La Habra Products made Anaheim the center of its hub, with corporate offices at 240 South Loara and a sales office and warehouse at 1631 West Lincoln Avenue. The Alhambra property became a ware-

house, along with other satellites in San Bernardino, Ontario, Goleta, Northern California, and San Diego.

In 1944 Nathan's son Chuck actively joined the business, as did Chuck's three sons—Fred, Terry, and Tod—some 20 years later. When Fred and Terry left to pursue other interests, and Chuck retired, Tod assumed the presidency. It was a major challenge for the young man, then in his late twenties.

"When my father offered me the top post, I said I would take it

One of two Anaheim properties, this company warehouse is located at 1631 West Lincoln Avenue.

as long as it was fun to do. Now, 20 years later, it still is," Tod notes. "From the start, I was determined to maintain the excellent reputation my family had established."

Tod faced a changing marketplace and new demands in the construction industry for products with greater diversity, environmentally

sound properties, and cost effectiveness. During the 1960s and early 1970s the company weathered numerous obstacles to become the widely recognized industry leader in the western United States that it is today.

La Habra Products' materials are used in residential developments and large commercial projects alike. Its staff has grown from 35 employees in 1969 to 150 employees today, including a number of second-generation employees from the same family, according to vice president E.L. "Ed" Fitch. The business has increased 10-fold, including an impressive fleet of 18 trailer trucks and 12 tractors, and adding both warehouses and materials yards around the state in Hesperia, Apple Valley, and Rancho California,

as well as an established business in Oakland that now also houses a small stucco plant. A new plant will open soon in Riverside County. Working through an extensive independent dealer network, the company ensures product availability at customers' job sites.

La Habra Products, Inc., continues to emphasize research and development to maintain its pacesetter image in the industry.

HILGENFELD MORTUARY

Not long ago, support groups in America's fast-paced society were nonexistent. One Anaheim resident has contributed to changing that by starting a support group for widows trying to deal with personal grief and radically changed lives.

Margie Hilgenfeld Field, owner of Hilgenfeld Mortuary and granddaughter of the establishment's founder, explains the support group as another dimension—and change—in the services her family has offered the community since 1927.

"I formed the support group, Renaissance, after many widows continued to ask for my help in finding insurance companies and filling out official forms," Field says. Now the group has broadened to serve any family member who is grieving.

For this and numerous other community activities she received an Annie Anaheim Accolade, an award given to outstanding local women. Field says she is just continuing the family tradition.

The Hilgenfeld Mortuary dates from 1927 in Anaheim, with two years prior to that in Brea. It was known then as Hilgenfeld & Rollins, its principals being the Reverend S.F.

Hilgenfeld, a minister and former pastor of the Brea Congregational Church, and Rollins. The partners built a reputation from the earliest days as prominent professionals, offering modern service and stately, tasteful help for the bereaved.

Its first mortuary locations were in both Brea and Fullerton, until the firm acquired the well-known Huddle Funeral Home at the corner of Broadway and Lemon in Anaheim. Rollins stayed in Brea, and the Reverend S.F. Hilgenfeld with his wife, Lydia, assumed management of the Anaheim parlor. As the mortuary's prominence grew new quarters were needed, so in 1940 the nucleus of its present stucco complex at 120 East Broadway was built. It was called the largest construction project of the year in Anaheim.

In 1963 an extensive remodeling and expansion program was completed, adding a chapel that seats 200 people and an adjacent garden chapel for private services of up to 50 people. The funeral home is one of the county's most spacious.

The Reverend S.F. Hilgenfeld remained active in the business until his death in 1966. His son, Melvin,

continued his parents' work, as well as his own interest in education. He owned the California College of Mortuary Science in Los Angeles from 1943 to 1977, and he founded the Hilgenfeld Foundation for Mortuary Education in 1978 to help ensure professionals the best possible training.

Margie Hilgenfeld Field began working in the mortuary as a teenager, answering phones and learning how to work with people. In 1970 she began to work full time with her father, Melvin, and her mother, Alma, who was an active force in the business for many years. When Melvin Hilgenfeld died in 1984, Field and her husband, Gary, took over the company and added a flower shop, called Melalma Flowers, in honor of her parents.

Their daughters Becky Areais and Cindy Field also have worked closely with their parents, and Becky plans to continue the Hilgenfeld legacy as the only family-owned mortuary in Anaheim.

The original Hilgenfeld Mortuary building was built in 1941. In 1963 an extensive remodeling and expansion added the 200-seat chapel and another adjacent 50-seat garden chapel.

CIBA-GEIGY CORPORATION

Aircraft primary and secondary structures are not what they used to be. Neither are interior cabin components. What once was made of wood and aluminum is now being created from technologically advanced composites—tough, lightweight, high-performance materials with properties that allow aircraft to do things they have never done before.

CIBA-GEIGY Corporation, with worldwide headquarters for its composite products segment in Anaheim, is at the forefront of the relatively new composite-manufacturing business. The industry has been compared to the electronics business of the late 1960s. Fueled by rapid growth in the aerospace industry and by increasing materials applications through imaginative research and development, composite manufacturing is quickly outgrowing its infancy.

"Use of composites for aircraft has evolved during the past three decades," says Juergen Habermeier, president of the company's composite business. "The good structural performance at reduced weight levels saves fuel. The lower energy content of composite structures—unlike aluminum—helps conserve the environment."

Another major advantage, according to Habermeier, is the longer service life of the products, the better dynamic strength that makes them more durable than metallic structures, and the improved crash and fire protection that may save lives.

CIBA-GEIGY is a leading producer of advanced composite materials, specializing in unidirectional and woven fabrics, "prepregs" or materials pre-impregnated with resins, and adhesives, as well as honeycomb core, structural panels, and fabricated parts for the aerospace, automotive, marine shelter, and recreation industries.

The company manufactures products that literally replace metal with structural composites. The lighter-weight materials have the equivalent strength of metals, allowing aircraft greater efficiency.

In Anaheim, CIBA-GEIGY's composite materials group has some 400 employees. They work in a largely self-contained operation that includes in-house research and development, project engineering, manufacturing, marketing, sales, and service. There are 150 more employees in Miami, which is primarily a manufacturing facility for non-metallic honeycomb core.

The company's presence has been strong in Orange County because of Southern California's strength in aerospace. As one of the largest composite-manufacturing companies in the world for such products, CIBA-GEIGY also was drawn to the region because of its emphasis on research and development.

The firm has deep roots in the county; it grew from a mid-1970s acquisition of Reliable Manufacturing to an international role today. The composite materials group has primary marketing responsibility for North and South America and is structured to interface with its counterparts in Europe and Asia. Locally it completed a major consolidation of 10 manufacturing, sales, and service operations at its Anaheim address, a 300,000-square-foot facility at 5115 East La Palma Avenue.

In North America, CIBA-GEIGY's numerous facilities contribute $3 billion in sales. CIBA-GEIGY Limited, the parent organization, is a publicly owned Swiss company with headquarters in Basel. It is one of

CIBA-GEIGY Corporation's worldwide headquarters for its composite products segment is located in Anaheim.

the world's leading chemical-manufacturing groups with member companies that produce a broad spectrum of products from pharmaceuticals to structural plastics.

The firm is more than 200 years old and has approximately $12.5 billion in sales worldwide. Johann Rudolph Geigy founded the company specializing in producing and trading dyestuffs and drugs of various kinds. CIBA (an acronym for the Chemical Industry Basel) was founded by Alexander Clavel as a dye house to manufacture synthetic dyes for silk. The combined companies have

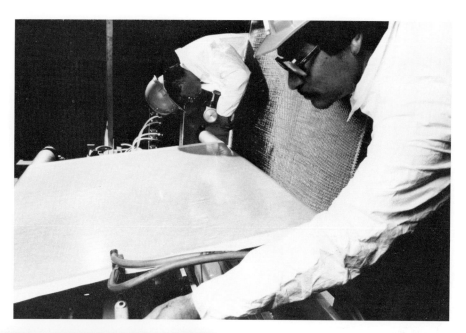

ABOVE: Where it all comes together—graphite fabric before film impregnation.

LEFT: CIBA-GEIGY aircraft floor panels are loaded into the press.

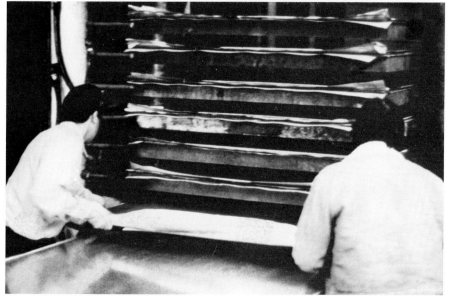

grown to a work force of more than 90,000 people worldwide, with major research and development, and sales units in some 50 countries. CIBA-GEIGY concentrates its advanced composite materials operations in Western Europe as well as North America to serve the major international aerospace industry centers.

The company exhibits cohesiveness among its composite group units by pooling technological resources in resin technology and fabric engineering to meet the aerospace industry's growing demands. It uses sophisticated manufacturing equipment and the

latest technologies. In Anaheim alone, state-of-the-art equipment and laboratories are worth some $50 million.

Product lines can be intermediates or finished components such as aircraft floor panels, and often they are structured to customers' specifications. For example, prepregs—for low-weight, high-strength structures— are used in high-performance aircraft and other transportation and industrial applications.

Adhesives, such as modified epoxy film, are a versatile bonding material for metals and composites. Generally high performance, the

material is used in the manufacture of large complex parts.

Honeycomb core, used as a basic structural material, is lightweight, durable, and noncorroding. It is used in aircraft, missile, space vehicle, and marine applications. The material is so light and rigid that it is used in creating beams, floorboards, flaps, and tail assemblies of commercial and military aircraft. Newer uses include road and marine vehicles, sporting goods, electronics, and construction.

Woven goods from all types of synthetic and mineral fibers are woven in-house in Anaheim. The company's variety of styles offers great versatility and includes twill, unidirectional, bias, hybrid, acoustic, and custom. CIBA-GEIGY fabrics have set industry standards, using space-age fibers and specialty engineering to provide design solutions for tomorrow's aircraft.

The international company of CIBA-GEIGY composite products segment is a fast-growing organization that focuses on forging new directions in aviation.

DEL PISO BRICK AND TILE CORPORATION

Del Piso Brick and Tile Corporation, a building industry supplier, has helped shape the community and in the process become a major force in the industry. The company has evolved from its brick and tile specialty, to a full range of masonry, tile, and stone product lines with supporting subspecialties. Today Del Piso is a major supplier of all styles and colors of brick, tile, marble, granite, and other elements used in the building trades and by retail consumers alike.

Established in 1946 by two brothers, the company was first called Anaheim Pumice Block. The founders, Jim and Louie Palm, recognized the potential of the area and put together an enterprise that would help meet the demand for building supplies by manufacturing concrete block. In the family owned and operated effort, Louie managed the business on site and Jim acted as a field sales representative and delivery man. At the end of a business day they would repair the trucks together. Their wives, Marilyn and Sally, handled the billing and bookkeeping, with first-year sales at about $20,000. During the next four years

ABOVE: Since 1965 Del Piso Brick and Tile Corporation headquarters has been located at 1635 South State College Boulevard in Anaheim.

RIGHT: Sally Palm, Del Piso president and chief executive officer.

additional masonry supply items were added, and in 1950 concrete block was discontinued. A more appropriate company name was selected: Anaheim Builders Supply.

When Louie died in 1959 at the age of 37, the company was on the verge of a major expansion as a direct result of the building boom in Anaheim and Southern California. Jim Palm moved ahead in 1960 to acquire Del Piso Tile, blend it with former operations, and create a more complete building supply and design company. Del Piso, which literally translates to "of the floor," became known as a full-service supplier of brick and tile, with a complete range of complementary products for the designer and building professional. At the time terrazzo was the Mexican tile of choice, and it was a great contributor to Del Piso's growth. (It is rare for a distributor to offer brick,

tile, and stone in one place, as Del Piso does in its various locations.)

Brick shipped in from other parts of the United States began to catch on, as did tiles imported from Italy and Japan as well as Mexico, so that by 1970 the company had grown to a full-time staff of 45 people and a fleet of 78 vehicles. Gross sales had reached $6 million.

At this point, Jim Palm, as chief executive officer, began another major expansion, and in 1975 opened the San Diego branch. Woodland Hills followed in 1978, and Mesa, Arizona, became the first out-of-state branch in 1982.

In 1987 Sally Palm took over her husband's executive duties following his death. Two months later, Del Piso's San Marcos branch opened its doors, and the following year a number of changes were made to better serve customers. The Woodland Hills store moved to a Sepulveda location, and the Mesa, Arizona, store moved to Tempe. Better facilities in more competitive market areas inspired the moves. In 1989, recognizing two rapid-growth areas, Del Piso opened stores in Riverside and another out-of-state location, Las Vegas, Nevada.

"We have tried to create a place where professionals are united by a

RIGHT: Before Jim Palm acquired Del Piso Tile, the company was known as Anaheim Builders Supply, Inc.

BELOW: The late Jim Palm founded the company with his brother Louie in 1946. Jim, pictured here, helped supply the construction of Anaheim Stadium.

common goal," Sally Palm says, "constantly offering better products and higher-quality service. That has been our intent right from the beginning."

In its 45-year history, Del Piso has gained a reputation as a major innovative force in the industry through new product development and an outstanding design-center display concept.

The company's steady growth has produced a current full-time employee base of 188 people in eight branches and a fleet of 15 semi-trucks. There are 28 outside sales representatives and 33 people working inside sales including at the order desk and

to install products, and its one-stop shopping approach has been widely accepted as an added value. Del Piso employees are proud of their company's penchant for quality and creativity, based on having one of the largest selections of building material in the industry. The staff is highly trained to supply both technical and design assistance to clients in all of the company's product lines. Among the company's specialties are ceramic wall, floor, and counter tiles from around the world, porcelain mosaics, handmade Mexican pavers, Italian marble, domestic and imported bricks, and landscaping and veneer stones.

Del Piso's large showrooms. "We try to maintain the spirit of family while continuing to grow," says Paul Muce, executive vice president. "It's very important because many on staff have long tenures here."

Del Piso has been headquartered at 1635 South State College Boulevard in Anaheim since 1965, remodeling and expanding its facility as its sales network grows.

The company markets and distributes products through a network of showrooms and design centers at each of its major locations in three states. Each center features a series of multi-design environments that pull display products together in finished vignettes with adjacent color-selection panels.

As a full-service company, Del Piso offers users all the tools needed

One of Del Piso's strengths is working closely with design professionals and builders in supplying materials for commercial and residential projects. Increasingly more projects are inspired by the environment and its natural beauty, with products honed to blend. Del Piso has developed working relationships with manufacturers who also have long histories, some dating back to the turn of the century.

The mission of Del Piso Brick and Tile Corporation is to continue the Palm brothers' ingenuity, especially Jim Palm's foresight for focused growth and ability to move ahead at the right time. The wave of the future, according to Del Piso's management, is not only in adding new products but creating new applications through fresh design styles.

JANET PARRY, R.N.
MEDICAL MANAGEMENT CONSULTANTS, INC.

Janet Parry (left) and her sister, Nancy Parry, M.D., developed their own medical building in Anaheim.

When people ask Janet Parry, registered nurse and licensed Realtor, for her business card, they have a choice of several: president of Medical Management Consultants, Inc.; vice president of Parry Development Company; partner in P&F Investment Properties & Management Company; or partner in Medical Billing Specialists.

It all started in 1968, when she came to California from Utah to help her sister, Dr. Nancy Parry, organize the business part of her medical practice. Janet Parry's intention was to return to her duties as a surgical nurse at Latter-day Saints Hospital in Salt Lake City. But as other doctors in Southern California noted her organizational skills and asked her to help them as well, she decided to stay and take advantage of the many opportunities in Anaheim.

Today Parry's primary business, Medical Management Consultants, is housed in the Parry Professional Building, the $16-million, six-story structure at 1801 West Romneya

Drive, one of Parry Development's major properties. MMC, on the top floor of the impressive black and glass building, is next door to Dr. Nancy Parry's family-practice suite. The building also holds some 75 other doctors' offices.

Janet eased into MMC, working half time for her sister (whom she calls "Doc") and half time in establishing her new business. "Doctors just aren't trained in the business aspects," she explains. "Paying bills, hiring and maintaining staffs, setting up a new practice, arranging the equipment, overseeing collections—that takes too much time away from their practice. Our clients happily leave all those details up to us." Now a full-service medical office management firm, MMC handles even the most confidential matters for its physician clients, including personal bills.

After 10 years of directing MMC on her own, Janet was joined by Pat Fron, a registered nurse and former supervisor of nursing of the student health center at California State University, Los Angeles, as vice president. Together they have built Medical Management Consultants, Inc., to five employees.

Parry and Fron's R.N. status is invaluable in understanding clients' needs. "There is just no substitute for having worked in operating and emergency rooms and private offices," says Janet Parry.

The Parry sisters (with Dr. Parry as president) combined their

expertise in health care with the legal skills of Susan Flandro to create the Parry Development Company in 1975. The partners' first major effort was the $2-million, 11-suite Medical Arts East structure at 1000 South Anaheim Boulevard.

Janet Parry's solid business background led her to become the youngest president, as well as the first female president, in the Anaheim Chamber of Commerce's 90-year history. She recalls her tenure in office in 1985-1986 as one highlighted by "tremendous courtesy and support" from others who served on the board with her.

Her credits include developing and codesigning Medi-Signal, a silent light communications system for medical and dental offices; authoring

Janet Parry, MMC president (center), and Pat Fron, vice president (left), consult with a client in Parry's handsome office.

a manual entitled the *Parry System of Collection Management for Medical and Dental Offices;* singing in the renowned Salt Lake City Mormon Tabernacle Choir; serving on numerous professional and civic boards; and teaching and lecturing for Nursing Education Associates when time permits.

ANAHEIM FAMILY YMCA

Mountain camping with canoeing and nature studies, martial arts with emphasis on self-awareness and self-defense, youth and adult aquatic and fitness participation of all sorts—these are but a few of the activities offered at the Anaheim Family YMCA. Activities are focused on teaching leadership and community involvement, but they are also geared to having fun. The YMCA is far more than a building with a lot of activities. Really, it's a way of life—a family atmosphere.

Still, today's modern facilities at 1515 West North Street at Loara makes the YMCA's diverse programs possible. Programs for youth and families alike dominate the busy seven-day-a-week schedule at the Anaheim Y, with choices such as Indian Guides, Indian Maidens, Indian Princesses, and trail blazers activities for parent/child involvement, youth and government citizenship training, and Junior High and High School Leaders Club. Participants of all ages—from preschoolers to senior citizens—take advantage of its services.

The Anaheim Family YMCA dates from 1911, when Charley Pearson, a young boy who later became Anaheim's mayor, rode his bike around town collecting silver

dollars to get the Y started. Its first program was the Hi-Y Boys' Club.

The first building dates from 1920, when a house on South Philadelphia Street became its headquarters, and a mud hole in the backyard served as a swimming pool. The outdoor baseball diamond was the first one to be lighted in Anaheim.

Milestone years for the YMCA came early. The popular Camp Osceola in the San Bernardino Mountains was founded in 1924; the National Council's charter and state's incorporation were official in 1930; and the girls' club program came along shortly thereafter.

ABOVE: Many parent/child groups such as Indian Guides, Indian Maidens, and Indian Princesses have long traditions at the Anaheim Y.

By the 1940s the Y had grown, along with the town, and it needed a new home—the first in a succession of several it would occupy before building the comprehensive structure on three acres that includes a large indoor pool, a chapel, a large multipurpose room, many individual facility rooms, a youth center, and the administrative offices. Phase two added a large gymnasium, an indoor track, four indoor handball courts, and two fitness centers: one for men and one for women. The YMCA also accommodates senior citizens, the disabled, and other members needing special attention. Anaheim Family YMCA membership is at about 3,000 people.

The first new building cost $70,000 in 1950; its current facility required major capital funds in excess of $2 million. John Crean, former Indian Guide father and founder of Fleetwood Trailer Corporation, contributed more than one million dollars, which made it possible for the Y to move debt free in 1972.

The Anaheim Family YMCA is committed to identifying needs within the community—then making every effort to fulfilling them. And that can only happen as more people get involved.

ABOVE: The Anaheim Family YMCA is a gathering spot for people of all ages and from all sections of the community.

LEFT: Happy chaos reigns as these youngsters pose for a photo session during a YMCA-sponsored event.

KWIKSET CORPORATION

Its product lines are almost too numerous to count. Its customers live in 50 different countries. And its reputation as industry leader keeps right on growing.

"As market share leader in our industry, we are constantly challenged to maintain our position, especially as the need for hardware and security products increases around the globe," says president John A. Lang, with Kwikset for 25 years. "Now as part of Black & Decker, we are experiencing tremendous synergies to meet those needs."

But Kwikset Corporation, which caters to residential and light commercial properties, has had a bright future ever since its founding in 1945, when Adolf Schoepe and Karl Rhinehart began a small lockset business in South Gate, California. The partners named their firm Gateway Manufacturing Company, and they set out to meet the stiff competition head on.

Their early product, a tubular latch lock set, did very well in the marketplace against hardware manufacturers' mortise or cylindrical locks. The simplicity of the tubular design provided an unbeatable selling point; it could be installed more easily and quickly than the cylindrical variety. That is how the tubular lock was advertised, and that is how it got its name of Kwikset.

The name, like the product, caught on, and soon the owners changed their company name to Kwikset Locks, Inc.

It took only two years for the company to outgrow its facilities with a work force of nearly 200 people. By mid-1948 a modern plant was constructed in Anaheim, and Kwikset moved its entire operation to Orange County to become one of the first light manufacturing plants in the city.

The company grew steadily for the next 10 years, and in 1957 merged with American Hardware

ABOVE: *Kwikset Corporation's headquarters and executive offices are located in Anaheim.*

RIGHT: *An assembly line for Kwikset doorknobs.*

Corporation of New Britain, Connecticut. In that merger the Anaheim operations became the Kwikset division.

For seven years American continued as the umbrella company until it merged with Emhart Manufacturing Company of Hartford, Connecticut. The new company became the Emhart Corporation, kept its headquarters in the state at Farmington, and it grew to become a *Fortune* 200 company with sales in excess of $2.5 million. During these growth years, Kwikset—the leading manufacturer of residential lock sets and deadbolt locks—expanded to Bristow, Oklahoma, opening a new plant in 1978.

In 1989 Emhart followed its predecessors' path, merging with Black & Decker, headquartered in Towson, Maryland. Kwikset, which has maintained its name and high-quality reputation throughout its corporate changes, employs 1,300 people in Anaheim for finishing and assembling, and about 550 people in similar operations in Oklahoma. A newly opened parts fabrication plant in Denison, Texas, houses 325 employees. Kwikset Corporation will open soon a plant in the southeastern United States to help meet both domestic and international sales.

YELLOW CAB COMPANY OF NORTHERN ORANGE COUNTY, INC.

The Yellow Cab Company of Northern Orange County, Inc., has been answering patrons' calls for decades since its founding in 1945. Its original name was Anaheim Yellow Cab, and its founders were the late Edward Slagle, his wife, Effie, and the late Clifton Briley, Effie Slagle's brother. The trio perceived Anaheim's potential in post-World War II years, with returning servicemen settling in Orange County and the area's overall development.

They began operations three months after war ended in the Pacific, working out of the Valencia Hotel in downtown Anaheim. But business did not boom immediately, and for several years the company struggled. The area stayed primarily suburban, with little demand for taxi service, and the operation barely hung on.

At the close of the 1940s, the company moved to its present site on East Lincoln Avenue and slowly began increasing its business. Development was finally taking off in Orange County as land prices and congestion increased in Los Angeles, and the company grew along with the county—purchasing competing companies in Fullerton and Buena Park. When Disneyland opened in 1955, validating the Slagle's belief in Anaheim, the founders felt sure their long-term planning would be realized.

Disneyland turned out to be a mixed blessing, though, because of a city requirement that the company put 10 new taxicabs into service immediately. The company complied and very nearly went into bankruptcy. But Yellow Cab weathered the storm, and in the 1950s it fell into a seasonal pattern: busy vacations and holidays, with slow winter months. That pattern continued until the Anaheim Convention Center was completed.

The 1960s were good for Yellow Cab, which added a major office and mechanical facility, and it expanded its administrative and vehicle service

capabilities. The company began operations in Orange, Garden Grove, Stanton, and Cypress, and it changed its name to encompass all of northern Orange County.

Diversification was the keystone of the 1970s, with Yellow Cab entering the burgeoning transit arena. The company contracted with the Orange County Transit District to operate Neighborhood Dial-A-Ride, a move that saved taxpayers' money.

Technological advances of the 1980s have been dramatic, and Yellow Cab has been among the leaders. It was one of the first to use alternative, clear-burning fuels such as propane and natural gas, put electronic meters in taxicabs, and install a fully automated dispatching system. Now Yellow Cab Company of Northern

Orange County, Inc., is diversifying into fixed route and group services through an affiliate, Western Transit Systems, including shopping-center shuttles and group service for the elderly, handicapped, and convention goers.

"We've built a reputation on being innovative," says president Larry Slagle, son of the founders, "and we feel we are well positioned to help provide ongoing solutions to Orange County's growing transportation challenges."

RIGHT: In this photo from 1961, Yellow Cab Company founder Edward Slagle poses at the East Lincoln Avenue headquarters.

BELOW: Tourism from the Disneyland area comprises an important facet of Yellow Cab business.

CARL KARCHER ENTERPRISES

The superlatives at Carl Karcher Enterprises, Inc. (CKE) are almost as abundant as its Carl's Jr. hamburgers. More than 17,000 people work for the company, some 1,300 in Anaheim alone. There are more than 550 restaurants in four states, as well as in Japan. Annual revenues exceeded $511 million in fiscal 1990. The company has reached its 50th year.

Carl's Jr. restaurants are owned, operated, franchised, or licensed by CKE, which exemplifies an all-American success story, combining humble beginnings with dreams

come true and hard work with perseverance. Founder Carl Karcher, born in Ohio in 1917, was one of eight children who grew up on the family farm. Influenced by his family's needs, he left school after the eighth grade to help his family. During the hard Depression years Karcher often dreamed of heading for California, and in 1937 he did just that.

Karcher went to Anaheim, where he first worked in his uncle's feed store, and then he landed a job as a bakery salesman and deliveryman. He met Margaret Heinz at church. They were married in 1939 and started a large family of 12 children.

Karcher began to work toward another dream. He had observed how popular hot dog stands were in Los Angeles, and in 1941 he decided to open one of his own—in partnership with his wife. They bought their first hot dog stand for $326.

Karcher kept his delivery job while he bought two more carts and hired two employees. Just three

LEFT: Carl N. Karcher, chairman of the board and chief executive officer of Carl Karcher Enterprises, Inc.

BELOW: This is the company's flagship restaurant, located at 1200 North Harbor Boulevard, in front of the corporate headquarters.

years later he opened Carl's Drive-in Barbecue in Anaheim and started his ascent into the restaurant business. With time out after he was drafted into the U.S. Army, Karcher continued to develop his restaurant, and in 1946 he made an important move—he introduced the hamburger to the menu. By 1950 he was doing a big business, and by 1956 he was ready to open two smaller versions of his original restaurant. He named them Carl's Jr.

Karcher added restaurants to his chain in rapid succession during the 1960s while he built a loyal clientele and a major firm, incorporated in 1966 under its current name.

The concept of upscale fast food blossomed in the late 1960s through Karcher's vision to offer service in an upholstered and carpeted setting. It proved so popular that CKE added as many as 45 units per year. By the time the growth of the 1970s peaked, Carl Karcher Enterprises, Inc., was ready to go public. In 1981 the formerly private firm began to sell stock to the public. About the same time, CKE moved into the Arizona market, having already expanded to Nevada.

Products at CKE have been pacesetters in the industry: salad bars and salads to go, 100 percent vegetable oil and charbroiling to prepare foods, and light and low-calorie entrées.

Carl Karcher Enterprises emphasizes two other important areas of growth in its corporate culture: comprehensive training and development programs for employee enrichment, and extensive community service involvement to help its neighbors.

MARTIN LUTHER HOSPITAL

Martin Luther Hospital's credo—care, respect, and responsiveness—has a new dimension. Through affiliation in 1988 with UniHealth America, MLH has added an extensive network of resources and capabilities to its roster of services.

Moving into its fourth decade as a community hospital, MLH continues as a fully accredited, not-for-profit institution serving patients in northern Orange County from its Anaheim location at 1830 West Romneya Drive.

As an affiliate of UniHealth America, MLH joined one of the 10 largest health care systems in the nation. Its former parent, LHS Corp., joined with HealthWest Foundation to shape the new system, combining more than 100 years of service to the community. Although MLH has no tie with the Lutheran Church, as its

name would suggest, its inception stemmed from a group of Lutheran ministers who saw a need in the community for a highly trustworthy health care institution.

The new UniHealth system provides diversity of products and services in expanded geographic locations. MLH, as one of the network's premier hospitals, participates in the Team UniHealth concept, which gives patients quality care at the most appropriate and cost-effective level. A prime example is the Outpatient Pavilion at MLH, an exceptionally busy facility that offers diagnostics, treatment, and surgery to help contain costs.

The hospital's many programs are based on the staff's sense of community. Among its top priorities are women's services (MLH is the leading birthing center for northern Orange County, with an average of 300 per month); oncology, with radiation therapy and hospice service; a laser center; and emergency room

In 1960 Martin Luther Hospital was a 138-bed, one-story structure in the middle of orange groves.

services, averaging 80 patients a day. Currently under development is a new program for prevention and treatment of child abuse.

Its association with LifePLUS, an all-encompassing drug and behaviorial services program, addresses some of today's most pressing health problems. Another well-known program is R.E.A.C.H., or Resources for Employee Assistance and Comprehensive Health, which provides counseling for problems ranging from alcohol abuse to legal matters for its own employees and for those of many contracting companies in the region.

The hospital also offers disabled and elderly patients easy access through a subscription service called Emergency Response System, an automatic dialing system that connects the subscriber with the hospital for emergencies.

From the start MLH built its reputation as an innovator and a model health-care practitioner, combining a friendly, personalized atmosphere with the most advanced technology possible. A 200-bed hospital with 500 employees, MLH has 40 departments and an annual budget of more than $90 million. More than 500 physicians are affiliated with MLH.

As part of "Team UniHealth" Martin Luther Hospital has a mission to "invent an architecture for the future" for superior health care.

Today, Martin Luther Hospital stands tall in the community with its 11-story tower and 200 licensed beds.

PICK YOUR PART

Glenn McElroy believes in a direct approach to business, and that shows in the name he selected for his company: Pick Your Part. The business attracts car buffs, mechanics, do-it-yourselfers, and price-conscious shoppers who are invited to bring their own tools and pull their own parts off the car of their choice in Pick Your Part's yards.

McElroy as president oversees four companies, which includes yards in Stanton, Sun Valley, Wilmington (with two), Hayward, and San Jose, in California, and one yard in Houston, Texas. There are more than 900 employees, and the company is headquartered in an impressive 14,000-square-foot building at 1301 East Orangewood in Anaheim. A fleet of some 200 trucks and 25 semitrailers move about 20,000 scrapped, abandoned, or unwanted cars a month in California alone to meet customer needs. In fact, Pick Your Part is known as the world's largest self-service auto recyclers of low-price used auto parts.

An interest in cars runs in the family. McElroy's grandfather and father before him were auto and equipment dealers, and he got an early start as "lot boy," washing vehicles. He established Pick Your

The Spirit of Anaheim, a 1936 Buick Century four-door sedan, is Pick Your Part's annual entry in the cross-country Great American Race for antique cars.

Part in 1979 as an outgrowth of a prior venture, an auto-wrecking company in Wilmington that dates from 1972. He started out with his wife and one employee, working in an 8-foot by 12-foot office.

After McElroy completed one year of business, he decided to advertise on television for the first time. The result, McElroy remembers, was so great that it was a near disaster. "Here we were with a very popular concept that got such great response that it broke down every system we had in place to serve our customers," he explains. "We doubled our customer count from 600 to 1,200 overnight."

After catching up with the demand and its ability to provide parts consistently, Pick Your Part built a solid reputation as "truly a good deal," says McElroy.

Today the yards are open seven days a week. ("In attendance, we outdraw the Rams," McElroy quips.) Customers pay a one dollar admission fee and a standard charge for parts. For example, the same inexpensive price tag is used for all fenders— whether on a Cadillac or a Pinto—as the business is based on volume.

The company buys its cars at auction from customers and towing companies. After the cars are stripped of all productive parts, they become scrap metal, once a mainstay but now a sideline for the company. The concept has revolutionized the industry through its massive recycling.

Towing is now an important part of the business; it ensures a supply for its yards and provides diversity. The City of San Francisco is a major contract.

Each year the company's Race and Show Car Division participates in the cross-country Great American Race, with Pick Your Part's *Spirit of Anaheim,* a 1936 Buick Century. (The division also has a jet-propelled car.)

Pick Your Part expects to expand to 50 lots in the near future, as its business continues to set new records both in admissions to the yards and parts sales.

Pick Your Part Auto Recyclers' corporate office, located in Anaheim.

KDOC-TV 56

Orange County's own commercial TV station, now highly visible from its base in Anaheim, was some 14 years in the making. It took that many years of discussion with the Federal Communications Commission to gain access to the much-sought-after channel and to establish the station before it hit the air in 1982.

Calvin Brack, the station's general manager and partner (left), has some fun with Pat Boone, station president and partner, at KDOC-TV's grand opening ceremony on October 2, 1982.

KDOC-TV 56, as an independent commercial UHF television station, won the rights over five fierce competitors. It is licensed in Anaheim and part of the Los Angeles television market, the second largest in the nation. Linked with a number of cable companies, the station is capable of reaching 10 million viewers in Orange, Riverside, and San Bernardino counties as well as a major portion of Los Angeles County.

Much of the young station's history belongs to its pre-broadcast days. Its owners, Golden Orange Broadcasting—including celebrity investors Pat Boone, Fess Parker, and the late Jimmy Durante—filed with

the FCC in 1968. Construction did not begin until 1975.

Golden Orange won its 1982 air rights largely on the strength of its community affairs and family-oriented programming in sports, entertainment, and public service topics.

"Forward to the Past" explains the station's current practice of running top-rated syndicated shows, including off-network and former CBS offerings. KDOC's programming plays to an audience that enjoys classic movies, nostalgic comedies ("The Dick Van Dyke Show," "The Mary Tyler Moore Show," and "Hogan's Heroes"), and classic dramas ("Perry Mason").

In February 1989 KDOC-TV 56 helped Orange County celebrate its 100th birthday by launching a nightly newscast. "NewsWatch" incorporates local news, weather, and sports with a news feed from CNN on national and international events. As the county's identity has matured, so has its need for local news. Sports was an important part

of KDOC-TV's mix in the beginning, and figures high on the list of ongoing plans as well, with more county and area teams slated for coverage.

But perhaps the station's greatest current goal is to become the area's health station. "The dynamics of an older America call for more information," says general manager and part owner Calvin Brack. "KDOC feels it's time to help create a greater public awareness on all aspects of health."

As part of its health programming, the station runs vignettes of medical tips called "Health Breaks" throughout the day and offers special programs on topical health issues. Weight loss, smoking, heart disease, child care, accidents, and sunburn are headliners, with experts joining in the discussions. The station also participates in community events where hands-on testing and health education take place.

The offices of KDOC-TV 56 are at 1730 South Clementine Street in Anaheim. Its transmitter is located on the 6,000-foot Sunset Ridge in the San Bernardino Mountains.

Orange County "NewsWatch" anchors Pat Matthews (left) and Michelle Merker help make KDOC's nightly newscast a success.

MONSANTO CHEMICAL COMPANY

Monsanto has long been a household name—in the yard, car, garage, laundry room, clothes closet, kitchen, bathroom, living room, and study. That is because Monsanto Chemical Company's numerous products range from swimming pool disinfectant to stain-resistant carpet to sweetener for food and drink.

In Anaheim the company's facility manufactures and distributes Fome-Cor® board to domestic and international customers. Fome-Cor® is a polystyrene foam laminated between sheets of liner board that has three primary applications: housing, graphic arts, and automotive uses.

"We developed the product in a joint venture with the St. Regis Paper Company in 1954 in New York and Massachusetts," explains Richard L. Faulkner, superintendent of personnel for Monsanto in Anaheim. "Now it is our mainstay in this locale."

In 1956 Monsanto and St. Regis installed the first major Fome-Cor® operations in Cincinnati, Ohio—a facility that Monsanto took over three years later. It continues as the company's only other domestic plant for the product, along with the strategically located Anaheim unit, which is positioned to serve primary customers such as Ford Motor Company, United Technologies, graphic-arts distributors, and the housing industry in the United States, Australia, and Europe.

While Fome-Cor® has evolved to be Anaheim's only plant process today, that was not always the case. The Anaheim facility dates from 1960, when the first half of the structure was built on an 18.5-acre site. It housed Monsanto's blow molding operation, which produced plastic bottles for detergent, pharmaceuticals, and personal-care products. The plant went on line in January 1961 under the name of the Plax Corporation, and it was jointly owned by Monsanto Company and Emhart Manufacturing.

In 1962 the facility became a wholly owned subsidiary of Monsanto. The following year the site was expanded significantly with a new facility to manufacture and warehouse blown polyethelene film sheeting. By 1965, still in an expansion mode, Monsanto acquired an additional 14.5 acres adjacent to the site. The company added another product, garden hoses, to its list in the late 1960s.

RIGHT: While it was exhibited at Disneyland from 1957 to 1967, Monsanto's popular "House of the Future" was admired by 18 million visitors.

BELOW: Monsanto's 67,000-square-foot Anaheim facility dates from 1960, when the first half of the plant was built on 18.5 acres.

Monsanto Chemical Company's Anaheim plant produces the polystyrene foam laminated board known as Fome-Cor® at this facility, which includes an area for production, a finished-goods storage area, and a yard for raw materials.

Major warehousing expansion continued into the early 1970s, first with film then blown-ware products. It was not until 1973 that the Fome-Cor® operations came to Monsanto's Orange County site and flourished in its three major applications. In the automotive industry it is used as a substrate for headliners, the ceilings inside cars and trucks. In the graphic-arts industry, Fome-Cor® is used for mounting photos and as backing material for posters and a wide variety of display materials. In manufactured housing, recreational vehicles, and home improvements it is used as an insulating material, creating a barrier against wind, moisture, and sound.

With its unique properties, Fome-Cor® enjoyed substantial growth in the automotive and graphic-art markets. Its popularity led to further expansion of the Anaheim plant in 1976. Several years later, however, the company redirected its manufacturing efforts, emphasizing select processes while divesting others.

Monsanto sold some of its local acreage, which was developed into an industrial park. Then the firm discontinued its film production in 1985 and divested its blown-ware business in 1987.

Further reorganization brought the Fome-Cor® business group into the newly combined fibers and engineered products division, kept its manufacturing site the same, and moved administrative offices virtually around the corner to 1339 South Allec Street. Some 48 employees work at the 5-acre facility, which is near the Santa Ana Freeway at Katella in southern Anaheim.

In addition to Fome-Cor®, the engineered products group includes Monsanto Enviro-Chem Systems; Astroturf® doormats; and Hydraway®, a drainage system for highways, golf courses, and building foundations.

The fibers division is growing through new markets and product extensions for its successful franchise operations. Basic fibers both sustain the division and offer new applications. For example, nylon—a 50-year-old product—continues to be vibrant. Product innovations such as the branded Wear-Dated StainBlocker program boosted carpet sales significantly when it was introduced. And new technology developments continue to extend product use.

The parent Monsanto Company, with worldwide headquarters in St. Louis, was founded in 1901 by John F. Queeny. The company's first product was saccharine. Fittingly, one of its main companies today is the NutraSweet Company, a remarkable success story that since 1981 has grown from zero sales to nearly three-quarters of a billion dollars. The sweetener, which offers the taste of sugar with virtually no calories, is one of the most successful new food ingredients in history.

Today's company also includes Fisher Controls International, Inc., which makes automated control valves, instrumentation systems and measurement instruments; Monsanto Chemical Company; Monsanto Agricultural Company; G.D. Searle & Co. pharmaceuticals; and Monsanto Electronic Materials Company. There are 43 domestic plant locations, a company presence in 52 countries around the globe from Argentina to Zambia, and 49,000 employees.

Monsanto creations have been showcased at Disneyland for years. The popular "House of the Future" in Tomorrowland from 1957 to 1967 had 18 million people tour its premises; and the imaginative "Trip Through Inner Space" took viewers on a ride through simulated blood vessels.

Monsanto Chemical Company's approach—in business and community involvement—continues to target improving the quality of life.

ARNOLD CONSTRUCTION COMPANY

Shopping-center developer Arnold Construction Company is truly a family business. Owner and founder Arnold Feuerstein is president of the Anaheim-based firm; his brother, James, serves as secretary; his son, Elliot, is vice president, overseeing the 800-acre Mira Mesa development in San Diego; and his son-in-law, Richard Rudolph, is vice president, with responsibility for the Brookhurst Shopping Center, which houses the company's headquarters at 2293 West Ball Road.

The company was founded in 1947, during California's post-World War II glory years, to develop construction projects in Los Angeles, San Diego, and later East Anaheim. "Everybody needed a house then," says Arnold Feuerstein. Residential development predominated until about 1954, when Anaheim opportunities accelerated, and the company switched to commercial development—its specialty ever since.

It was in Anaheim that Arnold Construction Company built its reputation as a community shopping-center developer, building projects of about 200,000 square feet. Among them are the Brookhurst Shopping Center (at Ball) with its 54 tenants, and Euclid Center (at Katella) developed in 1967. The company also built the 50-unit Anaheim Motor Lodge. "This kind of business requires hard work and good luck to prosper," says Feuerstein. "It has been our good fortune to be located in Anaheim with its exceptional growth potential."

The Brookhurst Shopping Center is one of Arnold Construction Company's high-profile development projects.

APPAREL
Cal T-Shirt & Apparel
The Right Price
The 5-Dollar Clothing Store
Kids Mart
ClothesTime
Lucky Fashions

BARBER/BEAUTY SALONS
Image Hair Styling
Macho's Hair Design

BEAUTY SUPPLIES
Anaheim Beauty Supply

CARDS & GIFTS
Bina's Hallmark

DRUG & SUNDRIES
Hill Drug Store

ENTERTAINMENT
Brookhurst 6 Theaters

FABRICS
Cloth World

FINANCIAL INSTITUTIONS
Bank of America
Standard Finance

FOOD MARKET
Alpha Beta Market

HEALTH & VITAMINS
The Vitamin Store

JEWELRY
Don Thomas Jewelers

OPTICIAN/OPTOMETRIST
A&B Optical
Dr. Sherman, Optometrist

PET STORES
Pets 'n Stuff

PHOTOGRAPHY/SUPPLIES
Foto Stop

RESTAURANTS/SNACKS
Arby's Restaurant
Bagel Traks

Baskin-Robbins Ice Cream
Howard's Coffee Shop
Jack In The Box
London Tower Fish & Chips

SERVICES
H & R Block
Joseph Tailoring
Launderland
Maletta's Shoe Repair
Post Office
The Weight Clinic
Travel Advisors
Your Valet Cleaners

SHOE STORES
Payless Shoes
Patrini's Shoes

VIDEO RENTAL & SALES
The Video Station

WIGS
The Wigfair

BROOKHURST SHOPPING CENTER

A complete one community shopping center only minutes away from Disneyland or Knotts Berry Farm!

Patrons

The following individuals, companies, and organizations have made a valuable commitment to the quality of this publication. Windsor Publications and the Anaheim Chamber of Commerce gratefully acknowledge their participation in *Anaheim: City of Dreams.*

Anaheim Family YMCA*
Arnold Construction Company*
Belanger Brothers Automotive
CIBA-GEIGY Corporation*
Del Piso Brick and Tile Corporation*
DuBois Towing*
Hilgenfeld Mortuary*
Dona Hinson, Realtor, Broker
Hoye, Graves, Bailey, Accountants*
Carl Karcher Enterprises*

KDOC-TV 56*
Kwikset Corporation*
La Habra Products, Inc.*
Martin Luther Hospital*
McMahan Business Interiors*
Monsanto Chemical Company*
Janet Parry, R.N.
    Medical Management Consultants, Inc.*
Pick Your Part*
Quintee Laminated Products
Seagate Substrates
Yellow Cab Company of Northern Orange
    County, Inc.*

*Partners in Progress of *Anaheim: City of Dreams*. The histories of these companies and organizations appear in Chapter 8, beginning on page 101.

This sleepy Anaheim street scene was photographed in 1898. Courtesy, Historical Collection, First American Title

The establishment of proper school facilities was a priority in the developing town of Anaheim around the turn of the century. Here, the first grade class of 1899-1900 poses for their class portrait on the steps of the Central School. Courtesy, Anaheim Pubic Library

Bibliography

BOOKS

Anaheim Immigration Association. *Anaheim California, Its History, Climate, Soil and Advantages* by its Citizens, 1885.

Armor, Samuel, ed. *History of Orange County, California.* Los Angeles: Historic Record Co., 1911 and 1921.

Ashley, Thomas J. *Power and Politics in Community Planning: an Empirical Analysis of Four Selected Policy Decisions Made in Anaheim, Calif., between 1945-60.* Ann Arbor, MI: University Microfilms International, 1987. Thesis (Ph.D.), Claremont Graduate School, 1962.

Booth, Louise. *One to Twenty-eight: A History of Anaheim Union High School District.* Anaheim, CA: Anaheim Union High School District, 1980.

Boscana, Geronimo. *Chinigchinich.* Santa Ana, CA: Fine Arts Press, 1933.

Carpenter, Virginia A. *The Ranchos of Don Pacifico Ontiveros.* Santa Ana, CA: Friis-Pioneer Press, 1982.

Carr, John F. & Co. *Anaheim, Its People and Its Products.* New York: John F. Carr & Co., 1869.

Freeman Bollman, Ivana. *Westminster Colony, California: 1869-1879.* Santa Ana, CA: Friis-Pioneer Press, 1983.

Friis, Leo J. *Anaheim's Cultural Heritage.* Santa Ana, CA: Friis-Pioneer Press, 1975.

————. *Campo Aleman: The First Ten Years of Anaheim.* Santa Ana, CA: Friis-Pioneer Press, 1983.

————. *George W. Barter: Pioneer Editor.* Santa Ana, CA: Pioneer Press, 1962.

————. *Historic Buildings of Pioneer Anaheim.* Santa Ana, CA: Friis-Pioneer Press, 1979.

————. *John Frohling: Vintner and City Founder.* Anaheim, CA: Mother Colony Household, Inc., 1976.

————. *Orange County Through Four Centuries.* Santa Ana, CA: Pioneer Press, 1965.

————. *When Anaheim was 21.* Santa Ana, CA: Pioneer Press, 1968.

Hallan-Gibson, Pamela. *The Golden Promise: An Illustrated History of Orange County.* Northridge, CA: Windsor Publications, Inc., 1986.

Jensen, James Maurice. *The Mexican-American in an Orange County Community.* Thesis (M.A.): Claremont Graduate School, 1947.

Kroeber, A.L. *Handbook of the Indians of California.* New York: Dover Publications, Inc.

MacArthur, Mildred Yorba. *Anaheim: The Mother Colony.* Los Angeles: Ward Ritchie Press, 1959

Meadows, Don. *Historic Place Names in Orange County.* Balboa Island, CA: Paisano Press, 1966.

Melrose, Richard. *Anaheim, the Garden Spot of Southern California.* Anaheim, CA: Anaheim Gazette Print Job, 1879.

Miller, Edrick J. *The Hayburners of Orange County.* Costa Mesa, CA: Costa Mesa Historical Society, 1978.

Musich, Patty. *Focus: Orange County 1990.* Balboa, CA: Metro Lifestyles, 1990.

Nordhoff, Charles. *California: for health, pleasure and residence; a book for travellers and settlers.* New York: Harper & Brothers, 1872.

Oral History Program at California State University, Fullerton. Anaheim Community History Project. Fullerton, CA: 1978. 2 vols.

Orange County Centennial Inc. *A Hundred Years of Yesterday.* Santa Ana, CA: Orange County Centennial Inc. and Orange County Register, 1988.

Parker, Elenora Alice. *Development and Growth of Anaheim Public Schools, 1859-1928.* Anaheim, CA: Colonist Press, 1929.

Legacy: The Orange County Story. The Register supplement, 1979.

Rinehart, Charles Herbert. *A Study of the Anaheim Community with Special Reference to its Development.* Thesis (M.A.): University of Southern California, 1933.

Schultz, Elizabeth J. *Famous Firsts in Anaheim History.* Anaheim, CA: Anaheim Public Library, 1983.

Walker, Doris. *Orange County: A Centennial Celebration.* Houston, TX: Pioneer Publications, Inc., 1989.

ARTICLES

Bell, Joseph N. "The Big A." *Celebrate!* Vol. III, *Los Angeles Times* supplement, May 21, 1989: 24-25, 68-71.

Billiter, Bill. "Divide and Prosper." *Celebrate!* Vol. I, *Los Angeles Times* supplement, May 22, 1988: 36-40.

Cano, Debra. "Disneyland: 35 years of magic." *Anaheim Bulletin,* Jan. 11, 1990.

Clements, Ken. "Anaheim Convention Center: A Fantastic Success Story." *Orange County Business,* Vol. 7, No. 2, (2nd Quarter 1973): 30-41, 43.

Dawson, Clyde. "Ku Klux Klan Once Operated in County." *The Register,* March 10, 1974.

Dodson, Marcida. "Anaheim: The Little Town that had Big Ideas." *Los Angeles Times,* July 6, 1982.

Emmons, Steve. "Anaheim Regime: Once It Was the Klan." *Los Angeles Times,* September 6, 1970.

Irwin, Kim and Penner, John. "Alpha Assessed," *Anaheim Bulletin,* series on redevelopment, June 19-24, 1989.

Jones, Lanie. "Blossoms in the Dust." *Celebrate!* Vol. I, Los Angeles Times supplement, May 22, 1988: 74-75, 166-170.

Kernahan, Galal. "The Travail of Klanheim." *Orange County Illustrated,* July 1965: 2-3.

Kimler, Forest. "Downtown Is Not Where It's At." *The Register,* April 16, 1979

Leabow, Jami. "Convention Center Plans Improvements to Keep Up With Competitors in 21st Year." *The Orange County Register.* Nov. 26, 1987.

McLeod, Ramon G. "A Marriage of Convenience: For Better or For Worse, Anaheim and Disneyland Go Hand in Hand." *Orange County Register,* June 2, 1985.

Melching, Richard. "The Activities of the Ku Klux Klan in Anaheim, California 1923-1925." *Historical Society of Southern California Quarterly,* Summer 1974: 175-194.

O'Neil, Stephen. "Their Mark Upon the Land: Native American Place Names in Orange County and Adjacent Areas." *The Natural and Social Sciences of Orange County,* Vol. 2. Natural History Foundation of Orange County, 1988.

Pritchard, Robert L. "Orange County During the Depressed Thirties: A Study in Twentieth-Century California Local History." *Historical Society of Southern California Quarterly,* June 1968: 191-207.

Reinhartsen, Bette. "Mechanic, 90, Remembers WWI Aircraft Factory in Anaheim." *The Register,* May 29, 1977.

Sharon, Clark. "Anaheim - The City of Muscle." *Orange County Illustrated,* April 1981: 43-55

Sleeper, Jim. "Orange County in The Great War." *The Rancho San Joaquin Gazette,* Vol. II.

————. "The Story of Orange County's Golden Harvest." *The Register,* Nov. 17, 1968.

Sterling, Sally. "Festival Grew From Diversion to Major Celebration." *The Register,* October 23, 1984.

Wroblewski, Annette M. "The Impact of World War II on Orange County." Proceedings of the Conference of Orange County History,1988. Orange: Chapman College, 1988

Index